MONEY SMART HAPPY HEART

Have The Happiness Money Can't Buy
and The Big Things It Can!

A Step by Step Financial Coaching Plan

CINDY TROIANELLO

DEDICATION

I wrote this book for you: to inspire you, to build your confidence, happiness, and security, to increase your peace of mind, and to guide you to financial stability and success. If you're in a relationship, I hope this book will help you find serenity and eliminate hassles and arguments about money.

CONTENTS

INTRODUCTION

If you had some extra cash, what would you buy?

I'm not talking about the little things, the everyday stuff that slips through your fingers so quickly you can barely remember it. Think big! I'm talking about the kind of stuff that sticks with you. What are your dreams? Would you like to have the down payment for a house? Take a trip to Europe? Safari in Africa? Snorkel off the coast of Australia? Buy a car...with cash? Quit your job because your boss is an idiot and take time to find the right job for you? Maybe you could just use a break and would like to take a year off. Do you need money for a wedding? To start a family? To have the wherewithal to start a business? Or would you just like to have that secure feeling that comes with knowing you've got a cushion of cash in the bank? And what about retirement? Thought about that at all? It sure would be good to know that you're preparing yourself and your family for the future. The good news is it can be done. And you can do it. You just need a plan.

It's not hard or painful. I know. I've done almost every one of those things mentioned above: the car, safari, house, business, wedding. I've done them all and, except for my mortgage, I've never been one dollar in debt. I don't have a huge income. I'm not a doctor, lawyer, or stockbroker. I didn't come from money, and nobody gave me a cent. I work everyday, and I make a living, just like you. I haven't denied myself the fun things in life in order to achieve these goals. I have just realized what it takes. I have a different way of approaching spending and saving, and I want to share this knowledge with my friends and with you.

I realized that it's not hard at all—I just needed to be strategic and master a few basic steps. I needed to understand where I was starting from, where I was going, how to keep my money mine (and growing) until I got there, and above all, *I needed to be happy and have fun along the way.*

I was able to keep my money mine because I gained a unique perspective on life and the world around me. I conducted my spending in a way that, although not difficult, only a minority of people grasp. I adopted a philosophy that made it all possible. Once I recognized how powerful these beliefs were and how they made my life easier and happier, I was able to save. I was able to achieve my goals.

How My Ability to Save Got Started

When I was 15, I wanted to join a neighborhood band, but I needed a keyboard. I wanted a Yamaha digital keyboard. It cost $2,000. I had a dream...but no money. I got a job in a local pizza place. From then on, the work I did was to earn money to achieve my dream. I opened a savings account and started depositing my small paychecks. They started to grow, and periodically I looked at how close I was to buying that keyboard. By the time I finally had my $2,000, the band broke up! But, at the age of 16, I realized what a good feeling it was to have a pile of cash in the bank. I continued to work and save, and by age 17 my parents came to me asking to borrow $3,000 to help them buy a car. Of course, I lent it to them. Being good folks, they paid me the same interest rate they would have paid a bank. As they were paying me back, I learned about bank "Certificates of Deposit" ("CDs") where you give some money to the bank for a set period of time and they pay you interest on it until it matures. As a teenager, I had no bills, so I could save just about all of my money and it was growing from the interest I was earning from my parents and from the bank. I was learning some very valuable lessons.

I lived at home when I went to college. I worked in restaurants throughout the summers, saving my earnings to pay for my next year's tuition. Four years later I graduated. This is when I experienced my second pivotal moment. I got my first real, full-time, professional job. I was so incredibly excited! I was screaming and whooping and hollering all over the house!

Then a few weeks later...I went to work.

My first day was a disaster. My manager was under a tight deadline and a lot of stress. She didn't want to train a newbie, so she didn't. She pushed me out of the way and did all the work herself. I felt useless and stupid. I went home and cried. For weeks, this same pattern occurred: terrible day at work; go home and cry. Then one day, through my tears, I made a terrible realization. It suddenly occurred to me that I am supposed to do this work thing...for 40 years! It was right then and there I made a vow. I reached a clenched fist to the ceiling and staunchly proclaimed, "WITH *GOD* AS MY WITNESS, I WILL RETIRE EARLY!" Well, that may be an overly dramatic re-enactment, but I did make that promise to myself, and a long-term goal was born.

I lived one last year with my parents and saved a bundle. The next year, I moved out, got a roommate, and continued to work and save. Although I only made $22,000 per year, I quit that job after two years and had saved $16,000 —enough to move to Paris. For the next year, I traveled, backpacked, and Youth Hosteled all over Europe and Australia. I came back with $5,000. My life since has been the same pattern: work, save, put some aside for retirement, buy a car with cash; work, save, put some aside for retirement, take time off to change my career; work, save, put some aside for retirement, travel for five weeks to Nepal and Africa; pay for a wedding; buy a house; etc.

So, I'm sure this must sound great, but maybe you're thinking, "Right. What didn't you do? You can't live a normal life and be able to save that much. You must have been a hermit. A miser. Wearing rags, and never going out to enjoy yourself." Not exactly. I went out a lot. I had loads of friends, and I went out wherever they did. I had lots of fun. I was active and happy and bought new things frequently. I just learned to be smart with my money. I learned to do the things in life that made me feel fulfilled, confident, and happy without spending, so I could put more away for the big things I really wanted. As you read the coming chapters, you'll learn how I did it, and how you can too.

Who This Book Is For and How to Use it

This book is for anyone who wants to learn how to be smart with their money, build up their wealth, be able to afford the big things money can buy, and feel fulfilled, happy and confident along the way. This book is also for couples who need to negotiate their financial lives, as well as their personal lives, and would like to be more on the same page with both. The exercises throughout are for all readers, and some are noted with special instructions to couples. This book is for people who have kids and want to teach them how to handle their money. If you model these concepts and pass on to them the lessons, philosophies, and techniques, you will be setting them up for a rich and rewarding financial life.

Whether you've got lots of debt, or none at all, you'll learn how to think like people who are financially successful, save money and stick with it. This book is for you regardless if you pay off your credit cards every month, carry a reasonable balance, or feel you are in a deep chasm of debt and your situation is so hopeless you're condemned to waste your money on useless interest charges for the rest of your life. If that's you, this book is the handle on the end of the rope thrown down to get you up and out of that hole. Grab on and climb!

You can read this book from cover to cover, but you don't have to. The chapters stand on their own, so if you are anxious to skip ahead, or go back and reread a section, you won't miss anything. The tone is lighthearted and conversational, but the content is powerful. If you are like me and hate to have to sift through pages of chatter just to find one or two nuggets of value, you won't be disappointed. *Money Smart, Happy Heart* gets to the point so that you can cover a lot, quickly. You'll get easy-to-complete worksheets so you can clearly see your financial big picture and understand how to set it straight. The exercises center the material around your unique situation and there are short vignettes that bring the concepts to life. It's a fast read and a lasting reference, designed to put you in control of your money, accelerate your confidence, and super-charge your motivation.

The Big Secret

At this point, I need to state the grand concept of all savings plans, "the big secret" that some books take chapters, or most of their text, to get to:

- Save 10% (or as much as possible) of your income, from now until you retire.

- "Pay yourself first" - take that 10% out of every paycheck before you make any other payments.

- Deposit your savings directly into an investment account.

- Then, forget you own that money!

I Know I Should Save...But HOW?

Telling someone to save their money is like telling an overweight person to lose weight or telling a smoker to quit. They know they should, but it's not that easy. There are plenty of experts who want to give you investment advice. If you give them just, say, $100 a month, or a few thousand dollars a year, they can turn it into a fortune over 20 years. Their nerdy little fingers fly over their expert-looking devices, adding up the hundreds of thousands of dollars you'll have. It's so simple. Great. You vow to do it. But, at the end of the month, or year, you don't have those few thousand dollars to give them. In fact, you may have an even bigger credit card bill. How did this happen? You can't invest it if you don't have it! Before you need help investing, you need help saving.

This book will give you detailed, easy-to-follow steps and specific, personalized guidance, as well as new perspectives and strategies you can put to work immediately. It explores the reasons why it is so hard to stop spending and will help you to become aware of, and overcome, the pressures you feel from society and your own conscious and subconscious blocks. It will tell you precisely what to do to be successful, how to stick with it and even give you proof that you can do it.

Do Any of These Sound Familiar?

"But I deserve it."

"But I can afford it."

"But I don't have the time."

"But I don't want to be cheap."

"But I'm young, I'll make more money when I'm older and I'll save then."

"But I just want it."

"But it was such a great deal I couldn't pass it up."

"But it's not for me, so it doesn't count."

You have just been a spectator on the sidelines of the "Parade of Excuses." These thoughts lead to actions that undermine your financial future. If you truly want to rise above your work-a-day/spend-a-day habits, if you honestly want to achieve your dreams and find some gold at the end of your hard-earned rainbow, you will have to overcome these spending pitfalls. In Chapter One, "Busting the Buts," we will look at each of these rationalizations in depth. You will learn philosophies and strategies that will positively change the way you think about your life, happiness, saving, and spending, so you can end up with what you really want!

The Plan

Your plan must do several things. It must point out where you are now, identify your goals and provide instructions on how to get there. Your plan will be a succinct outline of the steps involved in achieving your goals. By the time you are done with this book, you will have your own personal strategy for success.

The components of your plan are:

BUSTING THE "BUTS"! - Chapter One: Understand the stories we tell ourselves about money, how society keeps us spending, why it's been so hard to save and how you can turn this all around to your advantage. You will gain new perspectives that lead to more self-confidence and beneficial behaviors, so you can have what you really want.

DO SOME DREAMING - Chapter Two: We'll do some goal-setting for your money and your life. We go beyond your finances to discover the fundamental building blocks of a fulfilling and meaningful life, customized for you. You identify your material dreams and find out what it takes to attain them. Extensive data on happiness is reduced down to easy-to-understand basics that you can apply immediately. When you are happy and enjoying your life, without spending any money, you can put more of what you earn to work for you and end up having it all—fun and financial success.

FIND YOUR STARTING PLACE - Chapter Three: With easy-to-use forms and guidance, establish your starting place: how much you own, owe, earn, and spend. Then, you can play with your results, adjusting them until they reveal the plan that works best for you to reach your dreams.

TAKING IT DOWN - Chapter Four: Keep your money yours. Philosophies to live by, as well as strategies and techniques to help you save in a big way. Follow this advice and you will minimize your outflow, build your worth and get that good feeling knowing you're winning the war of wealth.

KEEPING IT UP - Chapter Five: Anyone can learn the "how-to's." Many can even follow them. But it's the winners who stick with it. Discover what's been holding you back and learn how to create long-lasting healthy habits. The seven simple steps model summarizes the lessons throughout the book into a clear, concise graphic.

INVESTMENT BRIEFS - Chapter Six: What do you do once the money starts to pile up? I leave the investing advice to the experts but provide a basic, straightforward introduction to investing terms and concepts.

That's it. That's all it takes to make you the one who pops off to Europe, buys your car with cash, sends your kids to college, lives in the house you've always wanted, feels that great sense of security from a sizable wad of cash in the bank and is the envy of your friends and coworkers. You'll be making them wonder if they haven't been vastly underestimating your income. Aside from all the extra money you'll find yourself with, and on top of the dreams you will finally make come true, you will also gain something else of extreme importance: respect. When you are in charge, in control, self-disciplined and self-confident, respect will naturally flow to you from outside and from within. Let's get started...

Chapter 1

BUSTING THE "BUTS"

Some people believe that when we are born we are all blank slates—everything we know is a product of our environment, that is, learned. Others believe that so much of who we are is innate. Regardless which you think, I feel there is at least one primal skill we are all born with. That is our uncanny and unfailing ability to rationalize. I am sure that there must be a gene in our biological makeup devoted just to this ability. How else is it that we are all masters of this art? We become experts at a very early age. Remember when you were a mere five years old? Your mother asked you, "Why did you hit your sister?" You were justified. After all, "...she was staring at me!"

Pick a subject, any subject. Why should I not go into work today? Why was it okay to cheat on my diet yesterday? Why did I claim those extra expenses on my tax return? We can justify all these behaviors in seconds. In fact, we don't stop at one. Rationalizations usually travel in packs—at least two or three appear at a time.

Question: Why did you record that extra hour of overtime on your time sheet?

Answer: Look, I work so hard for that company. They can afford it. Plus, I should have received a much bigger raise last year. Nobody really appreciates what I do around here. Anyway, I happen to know that Joe always records three or four extra hours every week. I only put down one.

We can rapid-fire justifications for almost any problem. Our arsenal of reasons why it's okay for us to spend money is large and well-equipped. Often, we secretly have a flicker of doubt deep within our heart of hearts. "Maybe I shouldn't have paid for drinks for everyone in the bar last night." This is the type of self-doubt that springs our rationalization gene to life. The more reasons we can come up with, the louder we protest, and the more people we can get to agree with us, the fainter and fainter that flicker of self-doubt gets until it is completely snuffed out. We are all experts in getting ourselves to really believe that what we did was the right thing. Often, we are so talented in explaining away our actions that we even begin to wonder why we didn't buy drinks for the whole building, even the whole block.

To make progress in any endeavor, you need to minimize the excuses for why you can't do it and focus on how you can. Saving money is a very attainable goal. You can do it. In order to hold fast against your rationalizations, you must first be aware of them.

You have two little spirits on either shoulder—a devil and an angel. One is young, immature, and always wants immediate gratification. He's agitated and jumpy. He has horns on his head, all the money from your last paycheck in his sweaty little hands, and even more of your hard earned cash scattered around his feet. He speaks to you as that little voice in your head telling you:

"Go ahead and get it, you deserve it."

"You make good money. You can afford it."

"Buy it, you don't have the time to do it yourself."

"You don't want to look cheap, do you?"

"You're too young to worry about saving. You'll make more money later, then you'll save."

"It will feel so good to have that, you really want it."

"It's such a bargain—you couldn't possibly pass it up."

"It's not for you, so it's doesn't count."

The spirit on your other shoulder is older and wiser. He is in a white robe. He has a serene calm. He also has cash in his picture, but it is stacked up neatly behind him—hundreds of thousands of dollars. It's your hard-earned and well-invested money. Unfortunately, he's mute. He never says a word. (How often do you ever hear a little voice in your head telling you not to give in?) But he is always there for you. He is there in the background trying to send you the strength and confidence you need.

What is a mere mortal to do? The devil is so strong and the angel is so silent.

These are the stories we tell ourselves that prevent us from getting ahead. You can put a muzzle on the devil and rethink these most common justifications so they'll work for you, not against you. Then you can get down to the real business of sticking to your plan and achieving your dreams.

"But I deserve it" - The Reward

You work so hard. There is so much stress in your life. You do your best every day for everyone else—your company, your boss, your children, your partner, your parents, your family and your friends. You stayed on your diet, finished a big project, gave a great presentation, or got an "A" in your class. When you do something good, you should be rewarded. Why? Because you deserve it. So you take that trip or charge yourself a present!

Our culture teaches us that if we do good, we should be rewarded. This concept is ingrained in us from the time we are very young and is reinforced every step of the way. A mother tells her child that if he is well-behaved she will give him some ice cream. Parents reward their kids with a larger allowance for good grades. If you turn in the missing kitten, you will get a cash reward, money for doing the right thing! The "good behavior equals material reward" relationship is widely accepted in our society. In fact, this correlation has grown from not only being accepted and practiced, to becoming quite expected. Whenever we do a good deed, we now anticipate our reward. This concept quickly evolves into understanding that we deserve that material token of appreciation. This strong cause and effect relationship guides us in much of our behavior and can even shape our lives. This belief is so powerful that when we don't receive some sort of tangible payoff for virtuous deeds, we feel that we are being punished; it isn't fair. If you work hard, you expect a bonus. If you don't get it, the company is being unfair;

after all, you deserve it. If you help a colleague land a great job, you may secretly expect some type of "thank you" reward—perhaps a small commission or at least a lunch or dinner. You hit your 10-year anniversary with your spouse. Do you expect a present? You bet you do! You really deserve it.

Verbal praise may be enough sometimes. But it's not going to sustain us for very long. Yes, approving words are indeed necessary. But, if we continue our worthy behavior, or perform particularly well, we will start to look for something more concrete.

Usually, we want our rewards from an outside source. We expect praise in a tangible form from our employers, our partners, or our parents. If we don't get it, we feel completely justified in providing it for ourselves. Somebody's got to take care of you. If nobody else is willing to acknowledge your value, you will. We even reward ourselves when we have already received recognition from the outside world. You have worked so long and hard, you finally got that bonus. What's the first thing we do? We buy a gift for ourselves because, of course, we deserve it.

"But I deserve it" - The Boost

Perhaps you've been through a particularly hard time. Maybe you've had some relationship problems, trouble at work or even (ironically) financial trouble. You deserve to be taken care of. You need something to make you feel better, like a nice dinner out, a great new outfit, or a fine bottle of wine. After all, somebody's got to take care of "number one," right? You deserve it!

There used to be an ad where a kid's hockey team takes a real beating in the rink. His dad puts his arm around him and gives him a Lifesaver candy. He just went through a hard time, so he gets a treat to make him feel better. When we were kids, we were happy enough to get a piece of candy, a special dessert, or our favorite dinner to make us feel better. When we get older, we usually graduate to more expensive comforts. We have been conditioned throughout our years that when we have endured a difficulty, a material gift will ease the pain. Some gentle words can help, but nothing works as well as a new toy. Now, although we've grown into adults, that same feel-better philosophy applies. The basic premise hasn't changed much at all. Have you been stressed out at work? Did your boss unjustly come down on you? Did you get passed over for a promotion? Maybe you lost a contest or you just had a fight with your partner. Whatever the cause, you don't feel so good and you're looking for a boost. Again, we'd prefer if it came from a friend or relation, but if that doesn't happen, we are forced to take matters into our own hands. Now is the time to treat ourselves to a high-priced dinner or do some serious shopping. Who would argue that we don't truly deserve it? Our society so identifies with this habit, we have slogans dedicated to it, like when you need a little "retail therapy." We even dedicate bumper stickers to it, "When the going gets tough, the tough go shopping!"

"But I deserve it" - When all else fails

Up to this point, we see that we "deserve" to spend our money on ourselves when things go particularly badly, or particularly well. Are those the only times we allow ourselves the freedom to buy based on the "deserving" principle? Not exactly. Have you ever driven through the ritzy neighborhood and, while you're passing all those beautiful mansions, thought to yourself, "Why is it *they* get to have all this luxury? I'm a good person. I'm always nice to people. I volunteer. I give to charities. *I* should be the one with the vaulted ceilings, home theater and swimming pool. Why are they so special? What did they do to deserve this?"

This is the philosophy we invoke that helps convince us to go ahead and make that purchase. You know those times when you're standing in the store, holding a desired little object. You're really not sure if you should spend the money. So you stand there, frozen, looking at your little item, examining every angle. This is the time your mind is subconsciously racing, trying to recall a rough time you've had lately. None come to mind. Darn. Ok, maybe you've accomplished a great feat recently. No, nothing to speak of. You did get out of bed this morning and made it into work. Uh, not really good enough. Ah-ha! You've got it! You blink yourself out of your catatonic state and realize, "Look. I'm a really good person. I'm thoughtful and kind...You know, I deserve this!" That was just the simple push you needed to make it yours. Ten minutes later you're on your way out of the mall, proud owner of a shiny new toy and that much further away from actually achieving any of your real savings goals.

BUSTING "BUT I DESERVE IT"

The irony here is that you do deserve it. You deserve the best that life has to offer. You are a good person. You do work hard. You're a trusted friend and colleague. You're good and generous to your partner, family, and neighbors. What you must understand, though, is that what you rightfully deserve is to see the fruits of your labor in a tangible way. You deserve to have that sense of well-being that comes along with that extra stash of cash in the bank. You deserve the big stuff. In fact, all those times you have used the above excuses, you've had it quite turned around. It is because you work so hard for your money and make every effort to be a good and kind person that you don't deserve to fritter your money away, ending up years from now with nothing to show for it. That isn't fair. Don't be unfair to yourself.

In Chapter Two you will determine your savings goals, your real dreams. You will be able to look at that expensive treat and see it for what it really is—a distraction from what you are really saving for. Don't stop the race before it's over. If you give in to these transient pleasures, you are actually denying yourself the things that have the true value: your house, or business, or once in a lifetime trip. What is it you really want? This is what you deserve.

If we think about it in another way, this "I deserve it" attitude actually goes against much of what we have been taught. It is an interesting paradox. On the one hand, we have learned all our lives, mostly by example and actions, to expect something in return for our good or generous behavior. However, our moral education tells us again and again to be a helpful, benevolent, and loving person without expecting material rewards for ourselves. Our religions and history teach us that the true joy in life comes from within ourselves and cannot be found in the checkout line of our favorite store.

Regardless of your particular religious or nonreligious beliefs, the Bible is one of the most widely read books in history. It is replete with stories of Jesus and how he lived by the three basic principles: humility, self-giving and love. It was not until leaving all material things behind and entering the wilderness for 40 days of fasting and prayer, did he become empowered with the Spirit. Christians are taught to live one's life in the emulation of Jesus. In this case, happiness would be found by living a life filled with good deeds toward others and devoid of material possessions.

Quite the opposite of expecting material rewards for themselves, the Jewish people understand that in addition to their other basic religious tenants, one should practice charity to those in need, actually giving away wealth to help their neighbors and those less fortunate. A wonderful old Jewish proverb says that the reward you get for giving is the opportunity to give again.

Hindus believe that enlightenment can only be found from within. Through the practice of meditation and yoga, which completely ignores outside riches and the material items it can provide, one begins to possess inner peace. And again, we learn that another great spiritual leader, Buddha, who was born into a privileged station in life, actually gave up all that he had to head down the path of illumination.

In other cultures, people learn to do good just for the intrinsic value of knowing that they are a kind and worthy person. This alone brings them peace and contentment. There is an eastern Indian philosophy that believes salvation can only be found when you free your soul from its material container, and matter spoils all that it touches. Spending unabashedly on themselves runs counter to their notion of selflessness and altruism.

Our international socialist neighbors are comfortable with contributing for the benefit of others and for the greater society. Examples of the benefits of extending, rather than expecting, can be found in many other cultures including Islamic, American Indian, and even tribal societies. Famous figures in our lives and history like Mother Teresa, Abraham Lincoln, Martin Luther King, Mahatma Gandhi, and, yes, even Santa Claus, teach us and our children the value of kindness, giving, and a life of service to others.

I suggest that we all take a little time to get back in touch with our moral roots and reflect on the philosophies of our international neighbors. You don't need to be paid for your experiences. If you had just made it through a rough time, congratulate yourself! You have come out a stronger and better person. If you have just performed a good deed, or achieved a difficult goal, celebrate! Tell your friends and neighbors. Get their praise and admiration! Do not reduce it to a material level where "you deserve" a prize for it. It's time we get back in touch with our "inner adult" and foster an internal sense of self-awareness, discipline, and satisfaction in our own achievements.

Think about the last good deed you did. Take a moment right now to quietly reflect on the goodness that is within you. Think to yourself: you are a good person. Know it. Feel it. You truly are. Do the same thing with your last achievement, and the same with your last hardship. You are strong enough to deal with hard times. You don't need trinkets to know that you are a good and worthy person. You don't need to lower yourself to a petty level of bringing money and materialism into it. Call up this feeling about yourself at any time, especially when you are most tempted. Practice this time alone with yourself in quiet contemplation for many good reasons, not just for the benefits of saving.

> There's great stuff piled on a store shelf.
> I looked at it and said to myself,
> "I know I deserve it.
> But instead, I'll conserve it,
> and increase my personal wealth."

BUSTING "BUT I CAN AFFORD IT"

Remember when you were out and saw that great jacket, or pair of shoes, that you have been looking for and really do need? Did you ever hear these words in your head, "Oh, come on! It's not that expensive—and I do pretty well. I'm *sure* I can afford this. Anyway, I have plenty of room left on my credit cards." And zooop! There you are at the register consummating the deed.

Have you ever been out with a friend when he slapped down the cash for a great new purchase? You have some idea of how much he makes, and it's not far from what you make; and if he can afford it, certainly you can, too. So, soon the two of you are in consumer heaven—shopping, eating, drinking, and having a great time. What a perfect day! You leave each other with a kiss-kiss or a slap on the back and you feel great. Then, only a few days later that awful, irritating, unpleasant day arrives—it's the first and rent is due. Darn. How did it sneak up so fast? And there goes the rest of your funds. You can almost see them flushing down, swirling away from you. You can almost hear the melancholy prayer music as you scrawl out that nasty, bitter check. Nothing left over to save again this month. "Well, my next check isn't that far off..."

Or maybe you keep your eye on your finances. You're not the irresponsible type that goes off, half-cocked, buying up the town. You have even made a budget for yourself. Perhaps it is not updated, and maybe it's not as complete as it could be. But you are definitely on top of your finances. You pass up purchases, use coupons, and usually order the least expensive thing on the menu. Yet, at the end of the month, again, you don't have anything left to save. Why not? It's so frustrating!

When you're unaware of your spending, or how to plan for the month, it is very hard to judge whether you are staying on target.

"But I can afford it." These words spring to mind easily and often. Do you understand what they really mean? Do you ever feel as if you're *expected* to be able to afford it? If you can't, it must mean that you have been irresponsible with your money, or worse, you are inadequate and don't make enough. After all, the more money you make, the more important and downright better person you are. Right?

WRONG!

Where do we get these messages? Why do we let them soak into our brains? You know logically that it's not true. How much money did your grandmother make? Was she not a good person? My grandmother worked on the assembly line of an egg carton factory. Not a rich woman. But I loved her with my whole heart. Look at your spouse, your friends and family. Do they care how much money you make? Of course not. How much do *they* make? What do you care? That's not why you love them. Have you ever had a friend who has been out of work or in some financial trouble? Do you care about his wallet? No, you don't. Then why do we sometimes allow our happiness to be stunted with the feeling that we should be making more money?

Life is the journey.

You must give up the idea that you will be happy when you reach your destination, when you make lots of money, when you become "successful." Life is happening right now! Let go of the false expectation that you should have more money and that you should be able to "afford it." You might not have all the money you want, but you are a successful *person*!

So, how do you know whether you can afford it anyway? Do you think that if you've got money in your pocket you can afford it? If you've got money in the bank you can afford it? Or, if you've got room left on your credit cards you can afford it? This philosophy is too short-sighted to live by. It doesn't allow for consideration of anything but the right now.

Question: Imagine you have no credit cards and you have only $1,000 in the bank. Next week you are going on a vacation that will cost exactly $1,000. Can you afford to buy $200 worth of new clothes for that trip?

Answer: Obviously, no. You may want the new clothes, but you need that $1,000 for the trip. You can't afford anything else.

It's clear what you can and cannot afford when your money is already earmarked. What if you didn't plan on taking that vacation, could you afford to buy the clothes? You've got the money in the bank... I suppose, giving consideration to right now, you could. But we can't live our lives this way. Do you want to take a vacation within the next few months? Will you need that money for anything else more important than new duds? We don't always ask ourselves these questions before we arbitrarily decide what we can and can't afford.

Perhaps you spy something pretty nifty that you can afford now. Have you ever bought something pretty good early in the month and then weeks later you find something really great? But now you can't afford it because you spent too much earlier? Fortunately, you will no longer have this problem. Since you no longer live by a fiscal policy dominated by right now, you walk away from the "pretty nifty" and later pick up the "really great."

Neither a Borrower Nor a Lender Be

Let's imagine that you have a close friend who is flat broke. She wants to purchase something for $100, but she can't afford it. She just doesn't have the cash. If you told her that you'd lend her the money to buy it, now can she afford it? Clearly, no. She's living beyond her means, borrowing from friends to get by. You may be willing to lend a good friend money occasionally, as long as she pays it back fairly quickly. If she borrows from you every week and pays you back in little token payments, stretched out over a few years, you'd get sick of it pretty quickly and would probably sit her down and have a talk about living within her means. Your friend's debt to you will hang on her like a weight and may even affect your relationship.

Now, let's get back to you. Do you ever find yourself a little short on cash but you still have purchases you want or need to make? Do you ever borrow money from a friend to make the purchase? Before you answer that, let me throw one more thing out there:

Sometimes Mr. VISA and Mr. MasterCard are our best friends. Using credit is borrowing money.

Now, do you borrow on occasion? Are you living beyond your means? If you use your credit cards to make a purchase because you don't have the money, can you afford it?

☐　Yes

☐　**NO!**　　　◄────────────────── (Hint. Hint.)

Every time you increase the balance on your credit cards, you are adding more weights around your neck. If you are increasing your debt to make a purchase, you can't afford it.

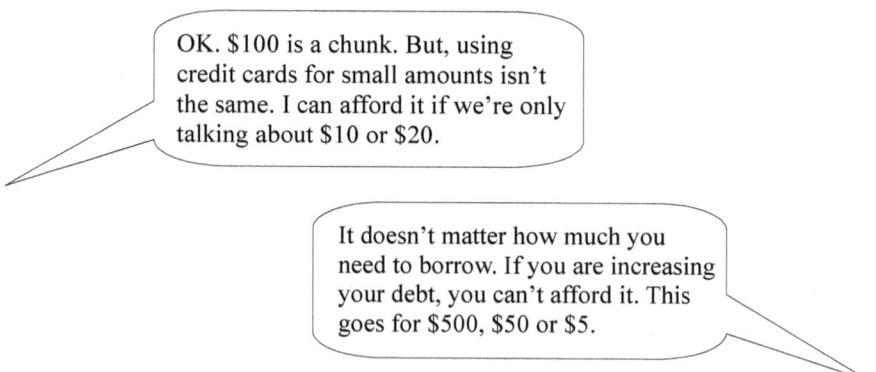

OK. $100 is a chunk. But, using credit cards for small amounts isn't the same. I can afford it if we're only talking about $10 or $20.

It doesn't matter how much you need to borrow. If you are increasing your debt, you can't afford it. This goes for $500, $50 or $5.

Is it easier for you to reach into your wallet and extract $40 and hand it over or whip out your credit card and slide it through a machine? It's the same thing, right? You're paying or you're paying. In a 2000 study, it was shown that people were willing to pay up to twice as much for the same item when using credit cards versus cash[1]. Does this ring true to you? It does to me. I know when I slap my card down I feel removed from my money actually leaving my bank account. It's just the *representation* of money being transacted. It's just the promise to pay—later. It's much easier to scribble your name on the line than part with your green. There is a psychology at play when you use credit, and it doesn't necessarily work in your favor. Keep this in mind the next time you reach for your card.

If you use credit and pay it off completely every month you're doing it right. Super short-term borrowing, for a month or less, means you won't be paying exorbitant interest charges and be subject to late fees. This is the only case where credit cards and the phrase "can afford it" may peacefully coexist.

Payback's a Bitch–An Illustration

You may choose to live above your means for a short time – it's a free country. You just need to realize that this is what you are doing. Then, after the party is over, and it's time to clean up, you will find that to pay off that debt, you will need to live *under* your means until you have paid it back.

Let's assume, for simplicity, that you make $1,000 per month. But who can live on that? So, for four months you consciously decide to live above your means and put $100 per month on your credit cards. You promise yourself that you will pay it back quickly, so you do not incur the wrathful sting of interest for long (and 20% interest is not unusual). You pay it back over the next four months. The chart below illustrates how much you will live on while you are using your credit cards and during the period you are paying them back.

Remember, you make $1,000/month. Look what happens!

Run Up Credit Card				Pay It Back			
spending per month				spending per month			
$1,100	$1,100	$1,100	$1,100	$896	$896	$896	$896
1st Month	2nd Month	3rd Month	4th Month	5th Month	6th Month	7th Month	8th Month

---

1 Study entitled, "Always Leave Home Without It: A Further Investigation of the Credit-Card Effect on Willingness to Pay" conducted by Drazen Prelec and Duncan Simester, 2000.

If you can't live on $1,000 per month, how the heck will you be able to live on $896 per month? You will have to live *under* your means to pay it back. Why is this so incredibly difficult? Because you are no longer used to a $1,000 per month lifestyle. You have now become accustom to a $1,100 per month lifestyle and you'll have to drop down to living on $896 per month to pay off your debt.[2] You may try to be clever and assume making the minimum monthly payments over a long period of time will get you out of this fix. Not so. Even if you make $25 per month minimum payments, you will have to live $25 under your means to pay it off; but then you are racking up more and more debt from the never sleeping, always growing interest. It will take you over a year and a half to pay it off and cost you almost $70 in interest—on only $400 of credit![3] Can you afford that?

The solution? Know what you can afford, live within your means and lay off the credit cards. Now, you're being clever.

---

2 Calculation generated using "Credit Card Payoff Calculator" under Credit Card Calculators at www.bankrate.com

3 Calculation generated using "How long will it take to pay off my credit card?" Calculator under Credit Card Calculators at www.fincalc.com

A Matter of Life or Debt

A private message to my friends down in the financial well.

There are many things you're really good at. Money matters is just not necessarily one of them. I bet no one has ever given you an education in the basics of money management: not your parents, not your teachers, and certainly not your employers. We go through high school, maybe college, and get a job. Then, a nice company hands us a little plastic card and says, "Go ahead. This is for you. It's fun to spend! And you don't even have to pay it back right away...just a little at a time...there's no rush." Remember how excited you were when you got your first credit card? The possibilities were endless! What to buy first? There was more freedom and happiness contained in that little plastic card than you could have ever imagined. You could buy what you wanted, when you wanted it: shopping, travel, dinners, lessons...anything. Life was good. You were happy.

Your balance started to mount, and denial took over; you still wanted to buy. "Sure, I can afford it; I still have plenty of room left on my cards." A few years passed and that balance got higher and higher. Now, your payments barely scratch the surface. You are starting to feel like you have fallen down a deep, dark hole—shivering at the bottom of a cold, wet chasm you can never get out of. Now where is that nice company that so generously handed you that first credit card? You know it is close by because you can hear the echoes of its sinister laughter as you pay down those never-ending bills, month after month after month.

But wait, don't despair! Look up! The sky is blue, the sun is shining, and there's a warm breeze blowing. Those are the winds of financial change, warming you up and drying you off. There's a ladder right next to you that you might not have noticed before. Put your foot onto the first rung: deciding to take charge and get out of debt. Then, the second rung: the exercises in Chapter Two. Pulling yourself up, you complete the forms in Chapter Three and commit to the philosophies and actions you read throughout these pages. A credit counseling service may give you a boost. You will get out of that hole day by day and dollar by dollar. Regardless how long your ladder is, I know you are strong enough for the climb. See you at the top!

Only You

You are a unique person. You have a particular look. You are the only one who acts like you and talks like you. You have your own sense of style and sense of humor. You have a distinct set of knowledge and experiences. Remember those dreaded high school days when you felt as though you needed to fit in and be like everyone else?

Are you still trying to fit in, or impress? Are you looking for acceptance, admiration, or jealousy from others? Are you driving a prestigious car that is stretching you financially? Do you really have the money for that club membership, designer suit, fancy watch, or bling? If you need to dress a certain way or project a certain something to get business, or a job, I understand. If it's an investment in the future, you believe it will pay off, and it's in your budget, then fine. But if you are throwing money around trying to buy respect, remember that your job, income, and overall financial situation are unique to you. You don't make as much as some, but you do better than others. You don't need to make a certain amount to fit in or to attract friends. Quality people, true friends, don't care about the money you make. Accept yourself for who you are and where you are right now. If you had some hard knocks along the way, recognize them and move on. Be at peace with your financial life. If you would like to change your situation–do it. But don't spend your money as if you are already there. That will just make it harder to get where you're going. High school is over, and you have graduated to having the confidence to be exactly who you are.

Yacht Shopping

Suppose you are at a dinner party thrown by one of your friends. Among the guests is a very rich man. It is not a secret that this guy is fabulously wealthy. During the evening he mentions his mansion, his ski cottage in the Alps and his four race cars. After dinner the group is planning to go out for a drink, but Mr. Money can't join you because the yacht store is staying open late waiting for him to pick up his 40-footer. Would you act like you can also afford one and go with him? Don't be ridiculous—of course not.

The next weekend you go to your company picnic. You spend some time with your boss's boss. There's no question she pulls in a much heftier salary than you do. Would you feign that your house is as big as hers or you have a membership to the club downtown like she does? No, I expect not. You can't afford those things. She's where she is and you're where you are. Everyone knows the score. You may be on your way up, but for now, this is the reality du jour.

A few weeks later, you decide it's finally time to trade in your old car and get a new one. The car dealership you're at has an enormous variety of vehicles: all sizes, makes, models and prices. Somewhere tucked in the back of your mind, you have a pretty good idea of what you can afford. But then there are all the beautiful fun cars you can't. As the salesman shows you the out-of-your-price-range selection, your brain kicks into overdrive, searching for a reason why you can afford one of these. You realize your good friend Jack has a slick new Z950 convertible, and he can't make much more than you. Your brain comes up with Deborah at work. There's no way she makes as much as you do, yet she drives a brand-new Road Rager. Hey! If they can afford it...

STOP! You're in the danger zone!

If you don't compare yourself to the rich guy or your boss's boss, why do you compare yourself to your friends, neighbors, or coworkers? Our modern hyper-sharing society hasn't exactly helped. It has spawned a new culture of compare-ism. Even if you are happy for your friends, enough posts of Costa Rican sunsets or bloody-Mary's at the Ritz can leave you feeling a little jealous. Truth is, you don't know what their situation is. Perhaps he just got a big bonus, perhaps they've been saving for years, or perhaps she is in way over her head. We all know people who show the façade of wealth and success publicly while they pile on the debt privately. These are not the people to emulate. Or covet. Like that last commandment says. Thou shalt not. I think a few of the seven deadly sins may apply here as well (greed, pride, or envy anyone?).

You can afford what you can afford. Look inward, not outward. Make your decisions based upon what *you* can afford, not by what someone else can.

...And Then God Spoke To Me and Told Me to Buy a Big Screen TV

Are you hearing voices in your head? It's not as wacky as it sounds. I hear them all the time. Often, they tell me: "Put it back, you can't afford that." But, before I had a clear understanding of what I could afford, they used to say things like, "That's not expensive. Get it. You can afford that." What do the voices say to you? If they start with, "Go ahead..." be aware. Recognize that you are trying to convince yourself. This means there is some doubt. Do you ever hear those words in your head when you want to buy a pack of gum? No. Because in that case you really can afford it and there's no question. Train the voices to help you out. Interrupt them and replace them with, "I know you'd like to get that. It surely is nice. But you can't afford it today. Be smart and put it back for now. By the way, have I told you how good-looking you are lately?"

I Really Haven't Spent That Much This Month.

This is one of the most common ways our funds flow. We don't think about it. We are scarcely even conscious of it. The end of the month comes, and we are shocked to find that we "...barely have anything left in the checking account. There must be a mistake!" So we go about double-checking the math... adding... subtracting...carrying the one. When the math checks out, phase two is listing off what we bought this month. But we can only account for a fraction of the amount spent. Where could it all have possibly gone?

Picture yourself sitting in a comfortable chair, having a lively conversation with a couple of friends. In front of you is a bowl of peanuts. You look down at the bowl, pick up a peanut, and toss it in your mouth. You wipe off your hands and keep talking. A minute later you grab a few peanuts, shake them around in your hand and munch them down. The conversation is getting enthralling, and everyone's voice is elevated. Within minutes of starting the discussion, you're chatting, laughing, and your arm has the muscle memory to reach down, scoop up a handful of peanuts and chuck them in your mouth without ever taking your eyes off your friends. The next thing you know, your hand goes nut fishing, but comes up empty. The entire bowl of salty treats is gone. Where did they go? You couldn't have eaten the contents of that entire bowl yourself.

Of course you did! You didn't mean to, you certainly didn't intend to, and you really didn't even want to. You were just unaware, unfocused on what you were doing.

Sometimes, we run on autopilot. There are some things we need to think about and some things we don't. Every now and then the "things we need to think about" accidentally fall into the "not thinking about it" category. Example: you're driving your car and you start fiddling with the radio. You look up and barely avoid sudden disaster! You swear to never again forget that driving your car is always a thinking activity.

When we allow the thinking activities to merge into the unthinking area of our brains, the results can be dangerous, even disastrous. To many, the activity of reaching into the wallet, extracting cash, and laying it on the counter falls squarely into the subconscious/unthinking category. This can lead to financial disaster. I remember admiring a new pair of shoes my sister purchased, and I asked her how much they cost. She told me that she didn't know. I assumed that she meant she couldn't remember, so I asked her to think about it and try to remember. She couldn't. Later, on my way home, I realized it wasn't that she couldn't remember; she simply didn't know. She paid so little attention (if any at all) to the price; it never actually registered in her brain.

MAKING PURCHASES SHOULD ALWAYS BE A THINKING ACTIVITY.

I am asking you to permanently re-categorize the act of spending (even on the small stuff) into the bevy of activities that you do in your most conscious, lucid moments.

Look at the price of everything before you buy it. If the price isn't listed—ask. Not listing the price is a game stores try to play. Maybe you won't ask. Maybe you'll buy their overpriced products without even noticing. Don't play.

Consider the price of everything before you buy it. Is it reasonable? Do you need it? Can you afford it? I'm not suggesting you sit down and contemplate these things. These questions can whiz across your mind in a split second. That's ok. As long as you give it some thought.

Can you list everything you bought this month? Some things will come easily: there's the rent or mortgage, the car payment, insurance, utilities, groceries, and gas for the car. Maybe there have been a few miscellaneous purchases here and there: a wedding present or a trip. But it still doesn't add up to the amount you deposited in your checking account this month.

The reason it doesn't add up is because that's not all there was. Did you include all the lunches you had out, the pet supplies, the daily cappuccinos or smoothies and the car wash? Did you remember the lessons, health club membership, haircut, and medical prescription? You may not feel it's important to include all the small stuff. After all, a cappuccino only costs $3.75. And you're missing $250.

Let's assume you're in the habit of grabbing a $3.75 coffee on your way into work and you work the normal 5 days a week, you have just sucked down over $80 that month. Annually that works out to almost a grand on coffee!

If you go out to lunch every workday and spend an average of $12 on your sandwich, soda, and chips, over three years, how much do you think you would spend? $4,500? $7,800? How about $9,300! I'm not saying you don't need a break in the middle of your workday, and I'm not saying you shouldn't go out to lunch. If you brought your lunch half of the days and went out the other half, you'd be saving over $4,600 in three years. If you invested that $4,600 and got an average of 7% per year return, at the end of 15 years, you'd have about $13,000[4]. That's good money. If you make it a lifestyle and took the amount you are saving by making your lunch every other day, $130 per month, and invested that amount *every month over 15 years*, you'd have over $40,000[5]. Now, that's real money. Could that fund one year of retirement? A year of college? The down payment on a home? Is the sandwich from the deli that much better than the one you can make yourself?

Reading this book should help to keep you aware of your financial life hovering just below the surface of your daily thoughts and activities. The Dream Cards you will make in the next chapter will also help, as will the activities you will do in Chapters Three and Four.

You may want to share with your partner, roommate, or close friend that you've started saving and you're going on a financial diet. Since any type of diet is difficult, you'll need all the help you can get. Ask them to remind you if you seem to forget, or are approaching a danger zone.

However you do it, do it. Don't just float along in a sea of subconscious spending. Grab your financial life by the bills and stay aware and in charge. Being able to afford it means you have the money (not credit) to cover all

---

4 Calculation generated using "What will my current savings grow to?" Calculator under Savings Calculators on www.fincalc.com

5 Used "Savings Calculator" under Investment Calculators on www.bankrate.com

your basic expenses, you are paying off debt, you have a cushion of cash for emergencies, you keep aside funds already earmarked, you are saving for the longer term, for the big things you really want, and you have money left over. Alongside this formula, you need to consider your future earning potential. What you can afford is a balance of all these factors. (The exercises in Chapters Two and Three will make clear what you can afford.)

BUSTING "BUT I DON'T HAVE THE TIME"

Do you get take-out instead of making dinner? Does someone else walk your dog, repair your clothes, wash your car or clean your house? Do you grab a coffee on-the-go instead of making it at home? How much is all this out-sourcing costing you?

Our lives are so filled with...doing stuff—speeding from one commitment to the next: work, spouse, kids, parents, friends, pets, cooking, cleaning, gym, doctor, church, lessons, birthday parties, homework, school, clubs. OMG! Take a breath! You need more time in your day. In addition to numerous personal, financial and business topics, I have been teaching time management and organization skills for years to diverse audiences of adults and professionals. Here is a summary of the points most relevant to saving you time and money.

Time Management

It starts with being strategic. "Strategic" means working directly and most efficiently toward a defined goal, beginning with the end in mind, and not getting sidetracked or distracted. Define your desired result in as much detail as possible, then work most effectively toward it. Know what you want, get what you want. You might have heard that successful people work on the vital few over the trivial many. They keep the big picture in mind and don't get distracted by falling down the rabbit holes of details that may be easier or more enjoyable, but will less efficiently lead to the end game. Companies create strategic plans to keep all of their management and staff moving in the same direction. Define your goal, draw a straight line between here and there, then get it done.

Limit Distractions

Turn off the TV, radio, music, and media, and give the current project your full attention. Ask others not to disturb you for a set time (for example, 2 hrs). At work, close your door (if you have one), or post a sign: "on conference call," "on deadline," or simply "please do not disturb until 3 pm." Put your phone headset on to discourage interruptions. Shorten calls and conversations. Bring your visitors to the point, "How can I help you?" and after a short chat, say, "I'll let you get back to it." Tell them you're on a deadline or you have a meeting in a few minutes. And remember, other people's emergencies do not have to be yours.

The Internet and all the fun, funny and ever-enthralling things you can find on it can suck hours of your time. It's the siren's song of distraction. Limit yourself to a reasonable time period, like 15 minutes, to surf Facebook, Pinterest, Twitter, the Internet, etc. When your work is done, you can come back and play. If you find a must-see video or have-to-read article, copy the URL, email it to yourself, then read it later. Turn off the beeps and chirps that alert you when text, emails or calls come in.

Prioritize. Do the most important things first. If you're not sure what that is, ask yourself "what impact will working on *this now* have on my future?" The task that has the highest effect should be done first.

If thoughts pop into your head while you're working, write them down. You'll remember them for later, and it clears up your brain to continue concentrating on the task at hand. Post a note to remind you of your objective or glance at your "To Do" list regularly.

Multi-task

Multi-tasking is getting a lot of news lately. The latest research indicates that our brains cannot actually process two important activities or thoughts at once, like driving and texting, or reading and listening. But we also know from experience that there are some things that we can perform successfully at the same time: watching TV and sewing, making lunches for the week and listening to the radio, talking on the phone, and...many household chores, like cooking, doing the dishes or laundry, sweeping, and putting away clothes. I know we all need downtime, but since this section is about finding as much time in your day as possible, if you find that you are less than optimally productive, do the kind of multi-tasking that works. Any time you are waiting (doctor's office, airport, train), add another activity (update your grocery list, problem solve an issue, read articles you've collected on your cell phone, plan meals for the week, take work with you, etc.). If you are lucky enough to have an hour for lunch at work, run an errand, grocery shop, read work journals, call to set up appointments, or catch up with a friend. Text to Speech programs are available that will read text to you (articles, emails, newsletters, Internet content), so you can consume this information while doing yard work, taking a walk or driving. Check your smart phone settings under Accessibility or install a program on your laptop or tablet. If your commute is long and you have a lot to read, this can be a huge time saver. You may need to prep your reading material first, like pasting what you want to read into a Word document. Speech to Text is also available these days and can help in composing emails, letters or reports in situations where you can't type, but can dictate.

Create Systems

If you have activities that you do over and over, yet they are less efficient than they could be, create a system. Break the task down into steps that can be repeated, in the same way, by the same person at the same time of every day or week. Systems could be created at home or work:

- getting the kids up, dressed, fed, and off to school
- getting dinner made every night
- prepping lunch for work or school the next day or for the week
- creating monthly reports
- preparing for regular meetings with your boss, staff, or co-workers

Enlist the help of others in creating the system and engaging in it. Make sure they all understands their role, write it down and give everyone a copy or post it where they will all see it.

Plan and Prepare

They say success is 90% preparation and 10% perspiration. Look at your calendar for the upcoming week and month. What can you prepare ahead of time?

- breakfasts, lunches, dinners and snacks for the week
- school, club, sports stuff for the kids
- choose outfits for the full week on Sunday night
- shower the night before when you have more time, instead of when you are rushing in the morning

Organize Information

Why do some people get so much done and others struggle to keep up? The "Doers" are super organized and are never without a few tools: their "To Do" list and a calendar.

To Do List: Write a list of everything you need to get done, then prioritize. Productivity skyrockets when you write it down, refer to it regularly, and tackle each item systematically. Write a sublist of what you want to accomplish each day.

Earn bonus time-saver points by making preparation lists for activities you engage in regularly, for example:

- packing for a trip (keep the list in your suitcase)
- prepping for a day at the beach or the lake (keep list with beach tote or lake stuff)
- preparing for a ski trip, picnic, dinner party, road trip, etc.

Calendar: Never miss a meeting, meet-up or birthday by using a calendar system to it's fullest. Add all the relevant information you need right into the calendar event, so you don't have to look for it later: the address, directions, parking, names, phone numbers, emails, instructions, links and notes. Learn and use all the functions available: alerts, alarms, repeating events, attachments.

To get anything done, put it on your calendar. There's the usual: meetings, appointments, lunches. Take your efficiency to the next level with the less obvious. *Schedule* work deadlines, project milestones, and simply *time to*:

- focus on your regular work
- clean, organize or file
- update your resume
- research vacation spots
- anything you want to get done, but don't find the time to get to
- any of the elements of happiness you'll read in Chapter Two

Anticipate instead of procrastinate: Look at your calendar daily to check what's coming up the next day, week and month. This will spur you to action.

Organize: Information is power. The faster you can get it at your fingertips, the more time you save. Your brain, as awesome as it is, can only keep a limited number of things in its RAM. Get it out of your head and in a place you will find it quickly. Write it down in an app, file it in a folder, or jot it down in your Home Information Book.

Home Information Book:

Fill a three-ring binder with lined paper and create tabs for different sections (restaurants, products, vendors, fun things to do with the kids, party ideas, Christmas gift ideas, favorite stores, coupons, warranties...).

Whenever you have a random thought that you'd like to remember relating to one of the sections, pop open your book and jot it down. Three-hole punch items to add to the tabbed sections such as instructions or large paper menus and include plastic pocket pages to hold loose items (flyers, coupons, or small menus).

If any one section gets too big, it gets its own binder. I like paper, but you can find an app if you want.

Organize Stuff

How much time do you waste searching for things you can't find? How much money have you spent repurchasing items you owned, but couldn't locate? Keep organized and you'll keep more time and money. Follow these steps:

Plan: Schedule time on your calendar to organize—a few hours after work each week, a half-day on the weekend or just 15 minutes at the end of each day.

1. Sort: The first physical step is to put your stuff into categories. Put similar things into piles.

2. Purge: Ask yourself, "How many of the same thing do I need?" "When was the last time I used it?" "Would my life be diminished if I didn't have this?"

3. Put away: Everything should have a home. If it doesn't, make one and always put your things back into their place. If you need more storage, scan your home for wasted space above toilets, on open walls, behind doors, and under sinks. Invest today in bins, boxes, bags, binders, and baskets, as well as shelves, cabinets, hangers, organizers, files and folders for big returns in time and money tomorrow.

4. Label: Since you probably can't tell me what you ate for breakfast last Thursday, how do you expect to remember what you put in that bin six months ago? Label everything that is not visible or obvious: on binders, boxes, bins, and anything that have been repackaged (travel liquids, pills, food and spices). Masking tape and Sharpie pens are sending you friend requests.

5. Keep it up: *Make some time, every day, to organize, and put away.*

Perfectionist Syndrome

It may be surprising to hear that many perfectionists are less organized and less productive than...good-enough-ists. They keep working and reworking their project until it's a shining example of the perfect specimen. They have a hard time making decisions, because it might not be the perfect one. They gather endless data, studies, and opinions, then end up with paralysis from analysis. If you recognize yourself here, take Queen Elsa's advice and just...let it go. Super productive people leave a trail of completed tasks in their wake. If your perfectionist tendencies come out on the job, talk to your boss. She may prefer good work completed this week over perfect work produced in three weeks. Try an experiment. See what happens if you cap it at "good enough" and move on.

Say No

Easy to say, harder to do. In her article in About.com, "Say No to People Making Demands on Your Time," Elizabeth Scott, M.S., provides a few simple but powerful ways to say no. She advises that you tell the requester that you'll think about it, take a look at your schedule and get back to him. Then later convey you would really like to, but simply don't have the time. A more straightforward approach is to be sympathetic, but clear and firm, and say when they ask, "I'm sorry, I can't right now; it just doesn't fit in my schedule." Then, change the subject or even walk away. Alternatively, you may commit to a lesser task. You can stay involved, but take less of your time.

What about saying no to your boss? Is that possible? Well, it is if you go about it the right way. Dawn Rosenberg McKay wrote a short article also published in About.com, "Saying No to Your Boss: Why and How to Say No to Your Boss" that gives great advice. If you are being assigned more work, try these good reasons your boss might understand. Explain that your workload is so large that even by working extra hours, either you still couldn't get everything done, or your other work may suffer and explain why. Make sure your boss is aware of everything that's on your plate. At this point, he may withdraw the new work or reprioritize your list so that current work drops to the bottom, or off your plate altogether. If you don't have the skills to complete the project, let him know. Just be careful, he might fault you for not having those skills, or he may expect you to learn them as you go. Tell him that you will learn these skills if it's important to the department, but they will take some time to acquire. She also points out bad reasons that will probably not go over well with your boss, like the project is too difficult, it's not part of your job description or you're too occupied or overwhelmed with personal issues.

All these techniques can be applied at home or at work. The more efficiently you move through your days, the less likely you will need to pay for conveniences because you will have more time to take care of them yourself.

Drastic Measures

If you are already a master of time and you still feel you need your costly-but-time-saving outsourcing, maybe you should consider something just a little more drastic: are you doing too much? Society pressures us to be super-achievers. You are important if you are in demand. You are impressive if you are needed, frantic, and don't have any time for yourself. But is this lifestyle making you happy?

If your busy life is sabotaging your future or the important things your life should really be about, maybe some of your activities are a distraction. Is everything you are doing making you happy—or directly leading you to a happy, healthy life? If not, eliminate. Even if they are all leading you toward nirvana, you still may need to cut something out. What are the one or two least happiness-producing things you are doing? Can you get rid of them? Everything does not have to be done now. Life is a journey—a series of events. As long as you are pointing in the right direction, you are on the right path. You can schedule things sequentially, instead of simultaneously. It doesn't all need to be done this year. Build in some time to relax, time to take care of yourself and your family with your own two hands, without overspending.

You might have heard an argument for doing the opposite. That is, some may say that you should delegate and offload as much as you can; you should pay to free up your time. Don't work under your pay grade. They argue that this frees you up to use your time to be more productive, and you can make more money with the time that you are no longer "wasting" doing menial tasks. In fact, I agree with this argument but *only* if you will use your time more effectively and be revenue (or happiness) generating. If your alternative activity to running your own errands or making your own lunch will truly get you closer to achieving your big picture goals, then I condone.

For those with kids, let's consider them for a minute. Are they over-scheduled or over-stimulated? Do they need to be busy every minute of the day? Can you decrease the number of expensive lessons and build in some on-their-own play or reading time? Would they benefit from having a few duties (that you now outsource) to help take care of the family like washing the dog, mowing the grass, or cleaning the house? You can help them build skills and understand what it takes to care for their possessions, pets, family and themselves. Let them help out and build responsibility while you cut costs.

Lunch and Learn

I was having lunch with a colleague. We were chatting about all sorts of things: work, husbands, fashion, our homes. The topic of cleaning came up, and she was telling me about her housekeeper. I casually mentioned that I have never used a housekeeper.

This stopped her in her salad-munching tracks.

She put her fork down, looked at me wide-eyed and asked, in all sincerity and genuine curiosity, "How do your toilets get clean?"

She almost got an ice-tea spritzer to the face from my busting out a laugh, "I clean them." Then I added, to keep the atmosphere light, "...but you know...I don't actually ever need to *go*...so they don't really get dirty, anyway."

Without missing a beat, she came back, "Oh, I don't either...but you know...the boys..."

Yes, I proudly clean my own toilets (though I don't usually talk about it). I know how the vacuum sweeper works and instead of dry-cleaning, I hand wash when I can. I sew up the holes in my clothes, and I wash my own car. It's not because I don't *have* the money. I just choose to put that money to work for my future and take care of my family and home myself. There is a certain zen, reflective, comfort in these chores. And I feel really good about doing them.

BUSTING "BUT I DON'T WANT TO BE CHEAP"

A good friend of yours is in town for a few days. He calls you up and asks if you would like to join him and his wife for dinner. They suggest "Maison des Couchons" restaurant, which promises a fantastic French dining experience. The problem is, not only is this place way beyond your means, you don't have time to arrange for the home equity financing it would take for you to eat there. Yet, your friend's only in town for a short time and you really want to see him. What are you going to do? Tell him, "Sorry, I'm too poor to go."?

How embarrassing is that? So, you suck it up, thrust out your chest and say, "Love that place! Meet you there at 8:00." Fine. You don't look cheap. Of course, it's going to make that part about you being poor come true... Anyway, what could you have done? You were trapped.

If you are keeping your costs down and watching how much you spend, you are being responsible and intelligent. "Cheap" is a label branded by others who are short-sighted and judgmental.[6]

Which brings us to the question your parents have been asking you for years:

"Why do you care what other people think?"

This might have been good advice when you were a child, but now there are actually many good reasons to care. Those "other people" are the ones who decide if they'll hire you, promote you, marry you, do business with you, or be friends with you. What other people think of you can mold your entire life. Although, you shouldn't be overly concerned with someone else's opinion, it is natural, healthy, and wise to care how others perceive you.

The trick, then, is not to necessarily change your behavior but to have it perceived in the best light possible. The easiest way to assure this is to simply come clean and explain your situation and not leave it up to others' imagination.

---

6 Why is it when you do your best to keep costs down and profits up for the company, you're seen as shrewd and clever, but when you do the same thing for yourself, you can be labeled "cheap"?

A Helpful Tip

One sunny Saturday afternoon, Kyra and Jackson took a hike and stopped in at the little diner at the end of the trail for lunch. Patrick didn't know they'd be stopping to eat and brought no money with him. After they ate, they realized that Jessica had brought barely enough cash to cover the food. They didn't have any extra to leave a tip.

If they had snuck out of the restaurant in embarrassment, there would have been one angry waitress muttering the word "cheap" in front of a string of shocking expletives while she cleaned that table.

Instead, the cash poor couple told the waitress exactly what had happened, and apologized, praising her service and berating their own foolishness. The waitress laughed and said that she had been in the same situation before, and not to give it a second thought. No one was cheap. Everyone was happy.

A brief explanation will save face in front of everyone: friends, salespeople, managers, business associates, family...everyone.

- Friends want to spend an evening with you, but they suggest an overly-expensive outing. Tell your friends, "That sounds like a great plan, I'd love to go, but I'm trying not to spend so much these days. How about if we..." and suggest a less expensive alternative.

- You're in a store on the brink of a purchase. The salesman who's helping you smells your intentions. He plays the "cheap card" to press you into buying the best and most expensive unit. Although we honestly don't care what salesmen think about us, sometimes, confronted with that well-practiced, smug condescension, we buckle. Don't cower from his manipulative innuendo. First, you don't owe him an explanation. But, if you want to, give him your reasons: "No thanks. The bigger one's not worth it to me." Or, maybe add some creativity: "I pay so much for my psychosis medication, I can barely afford the smaller one!"

Dinner Out With The Gang

Dinner with a friend is fun, but dinner with a whole group of friends can be a blast; you all share stories, laughs, drinks, and eats. Everything is going great until that awkward moment when the bill comes. Nobody particularly liked math in school, and certainly nobody wants to interrupt the party with a calculator adding up who owes what. So, inevitably someone suggests that you all just split up the bill evenly. Everyone agrees and the next thing you know, although you had only an iced tea and an appetizer, you're kicking in $30 to cover the bill. Then, what always happens? The person with check-duty says, "We're still a little short. Can everyone come up with another dollar or two?" So, you begrudgingly reach into the depths of your wallet and come up with even more money to subsidize someone else's gourmet meal. Had you known how this was going to turn out, you could have ordered the filet mignon, too. Of course, you couldn't possibly refuse to pitch in your "equal" share. This would make you look petty and cheap. Besides, these are your friends. What goes around comes around, and you'll have a meal subsidized for you someday. This is fine, unless you are always the one subsidizing the rest.

Wouldn't it be better if "What goes around" just kept going—and missed you altogether? There are ways. You don't need to pay for their champagne on your beer budget.

Dinner our with the gang is one of my favorite ways to spend an evening. Just because I'm trying to save money, I would never turn down a night out with my friends. You don't need to either. Nor do you need to resign yourself to subsidizing someone else's meal for the privilege of the experience. You must be aware of the potential problem up front. Your best defense is a good offense: suggest to the organizer a reasonable restaurant. Whichever place they choose, before you order, ask your server if your order can be put on a separate bill. You don't need to be secretive about this. It's fine to let your friends know that you will be on a different bill. You may ask everyone at the table if they all want to be put on separate checks. Your friends will probably appreciate your thoughtfulness and also want to avoid an inequitable check split at the end of the meal. When you take this route, you need to be careful that you don't share in the pitcher of margaritas or split the appetizers with everyone. If you share the food or drink, you must pitch in for it. But, if you only plan on having one drink, or just want a small appetizer, I recommend that you order a separate one for yourself. Usually, when the pitchers are flowing, people are consuming freely. It's usually not appropriate to split the bill for shared items in any other percentage than evenly between everyone, no matter what fraction you had.

If you forgot or missed the opportunity to have a separate check (or if your server refuses), when the check comes suggest that everyone takes a look at what they ordered and pay that amount. This is easiest if you are the person who receives the check for the table. You may want to remind everyone to include their drinks, tax and tip. If you're outnumbered and everyone wants to split up the bill evenly, tell them that you are trying really hard to keep your costs down and would like to just pay for what you ordered. You don't need to broadcast this to everyone at the table; just tell the person who is splitting up the check. She can take your amount off the top, then split the rest of the bill evenly. Who would fault you? You are simply being honest and fair. I usually put in an extra few dollars to make sure I've covered my entire bill so no one will feel that I'm not pulling my weight. These extra few dollars will be much less than the alternative of paying 40% or 50% more than what you ordered.

TRY THIS: To be sure you won't order too much, have a snack at home—half of a sandwich or a granola bar—so you're not so hungry at the restaurant. Same goes for the liquor, which is so expensive and disappears so quickly. Save the drink for when you get home...or have a drink before you leave the house, so you start out somewhat satisfied and not really craving the wine, beer, or cosmo. Just don't drink too much—I'm suggesting a little nip, so you are still safe to drive. And, when you're at the restaurant, have soda or iced tea instead of the alcohol. You'll probably spend a third of the cost or less. Then, enjoy your friends and the night.

...AND TRY THIS: Meeting just a few friends at a restaurant for dinner? Invite them to your home for a drink and appetizer before you go. With the abundance of good, inexpensive wine and beer in the market these days, and the low cost of making an appetizer, you can cut your dinner costs down dramatically. You can buy a bottle of wine from the store for close to the price of one glass from the bar. The bookend to this suggestion is to have friends over for dessert and drinks. Either way, you substitute the high-cost drinks for the low-cost alternative at home. You don't need to spend, spend, spend to enjoy.

Charitable Giving

We're confronted almost every day with someone asking for us to part with our money. Kind and needy strangers are constantly asking us for the smallest of donations. They are all so genuine and could really use our help. There are the clergy in the airports, Vets, Fireman's Fund, Easter Seals, anti-gang groups, blind, homeless, Save the Whales! To whom do we say "No"?

It's even harder to refuse the people you know. The nice people you are surrounded by—friends, neighbors, co-workers, church and community leaders. They have the unfair advantage of being familiar to you. Although you may sincerely want to, you simply can't support every friend or colleague's request. Yet, every time they ask, you are faced with the "look cheap or pay up" decision.

How can you possibly not:

- Buy her Girl Scout cookies?
- Chip in for the office present?
- Sponsor him in the charity run?
- Buy the candy?
- Donate to the church?

Here's how.

First, don't misunderstand me. Charitable giving is a good and noble act. I think the world would be a better place if we all gave something of ourselves regularly. Being generous and charitable does not necessarily mean we need to hand over cash. Donating a few spare hours each week or month to your favorite cause is not only very worthy time spent but is enormously appreciated by the recipient and is more rewarding to you than writing a check.

Maybe you don't have a few extra hours each week, but you still want to be a part of the healing and helping influences in the world. Pick a charity and make your donations. But first make sure that your generosity makes sense within your own financial world. The way to do this is to plan out the amount of giving you want to do ahead of time. When you fill in where your money goes on your Personal Spending Plan in Chapter Three, include the maximum amount of charity you feel is right. This way you'll have a handle on how much you can offer, how much you can truly afford. Then, when you have to turn down a request, no matter how deserving, you should not feel guilty. You will know that it's not in your budget, and you simply cannot afford it.

You now have the response you need for every Girl Scout, co-worker, or social worker. Tell them that you have a charity you give to and you just can't afford any more this month (or year), wish them good luck, and change the subject. Ask them about the event, fundraiser, or their involvement in the charity. Do this genuinely, without acting coy or guilty. They will realize that you're on top of your finances and in control of your own life and spending.

Let's see an example:

Eva is your good friend at work. She has just signed up to be in the "10K Run for AIDS." She stops by your desk and asks whether you can sponsor her for this worthy charity. She suggests only two dollars per kilometer. Look her in the eye and say, "Eva what you're doing is really great and I wish I could help, but I can't afford to give this month. Good luck!" End it with a smile and go back to what you were doing.

The Office Gifts

Sometimes we find ourselves spending money when we least expect it like those days you're at work, doing your job, minding your own business, and someone comes by with the dreaded envelope. You know what this means: Robert is getting married, Susan is having a baby, Ted is retiring, or Pam is moving away, and everyone is chipping in to get them a present. Then, that friendly co-worker who is walking around the "secret" collection gives you a suggestion, "Put in whatever you'd like. Most people are contributing 10 dollars." She may even stand there, waiting for you to cough up your donation. Whether you love the idea and have the money or are in debt and prefer to pass, it doesn't matter. You don't feel as if you have much of a choice. If you don't chip in you'll look awfully cheap, so you dole out the suggested gift.

It's not bad enough that your money flies from your hands for every necessary expense for your own home, family, and friends, you're expected to give up your own hard earned money at work, too?

41

As for those office presents for which you are expected to pitch in, first you must decide to whom you want to give a gift and how much. Do this without regard to how you may look, but decide how much you truly want to give, if any. If you can afford it and want to, then definitely donate. But, if you feel uncomfortable spending the money or simply don't want to, don't feel

bad. If the collection envelope comes around anonymously, you're ok, just pass it on. But, if it's accompanied by a snoopy coworker, tell him that you're in the middle of something, or you need to check how much cash you've got, and you'll find him later with your contribution. You may want to ask him when the deadline is and where you will be able to find the envelope. Now, you're in control. You've just avoided being put on the spot and can decide how much you want to give without having the pressure of someone standing in front of you. Put your donation in an envelope, then later find him and hand it over. Or, you don't need to go find him at all. You are not obliged to contribute to every office request. And, however small your donation, don't apologize. After all, you're at work to make money, not give it up.

If you've decided not to add to the contribution and the office "collection agent" is pushy enough to persist, tell him you're thinking about getting something individually. Then, either do or don't. It's none of his business what you do in this regard. Don't bring it up again. If he has the gall to ask you about it later ," What did you end up getting Tom?" tell him, "You know, I've been so busy, I didn't get a chance to get out."

If you feel comfortable, go to the big boss who can make this decision and tell her that these people hovering over you make you, and possibly everyone else in the company, feel uncomfortable. Ask if they can make a policy of pinning their cookie sales or sponsored sport sheet up in a common area with their name clearly marked. Then, people can go to them personally if they want to donate and no one has to feel pressured or uncomfortable.

A Note On Being Too..."Frugal"

I advocate being financially conscientious but not at the expense of others. Dishonoring the honor system, purchasing items to use once then returning, stealing, pirating content, or taking advantage in any way—is simply not right. I even knew a guy who took candy from his coworkers' desk drawers when they weren't around. This type of cheap-skating is an abuse. It also injures the integrity and reputation of the cheap-skate, whether anyone ever calls him on it or not.

If you aren't hurting or slighting anyone and you are making choices with your money that only affect you (and your family), do it with confidence. Then, tell that guy judging you as "cheap" that you can't see what you're doing because his big fat nose is stuck smack in the middle of your business and he needs to extract it. I'm pretty sure he's not a perfect person and there are plenty of judgments you could make about him. (But you won't, because you're the bigger person.)

BUSTING "BUT, I'M YOUNG, I'LL MAKE MORE MONEY WHEN I'M OLDER AND I'LL SAVE THEN"

"Look," you think, "I couldn't agree with you more. Everything you've said so far makes perfect sense. It's just that I'm too young for this whole topic. I've got countless years until I'm ready to retire. I'll make a lot more money in the future. I'll save then."

Let me ask you this: do you have more money in the bank now than you did five years ago? How about 10 years ago? Are you making more money now than you did then? At what age will you start saving? Do you have a date and time picked out? "At 3:00 pm on November 22nd, in 4 years, I will become completely financially responsible."

What is your plan on how to get to the place where you'll be pulling in a lot more money? Once you get to this place, will you continue to increase your spending according to your new financial status? Will you get married? Have kids? Buy a house? New car? When will you really be able to start your savings program?

When I was studying business in college, I had the opportunity to take a typing class. I snubbed the idea because certainly, "I won't need to type, I'll have my assistant do the typing for me." Now, all these years later, guess who's doing my typing? Although you can't exactly call the searching and stabbing, I do "typing." The best-laid plans don't always work out the way we expect. Had I invested a little bit of time up front learning this skill, I would have saved myself enormous amounts of time throughout the years.

This is your chance to invest a little up front and see enormous returns throughout the years. By putting a little away now, your money will start to work for you without you doing any work at all. This is the easiest money you'll ever make. You'll be making money while you're sleeping, eating and playing. You'll even be making money while you're making money. This is the concept of investing. You take some money up front from your paycheck, bonus, tax refund, etc., and put it in an investment and let it sit there. (Investment options like stocks, mutual funds, bonds, real estate and certificates of deposit are explained in Chapter Six, "Investment Briefs.") Your money may earn interest or increase in value; it starts to grow. And in your later years, when you're ready to retire, you won't even recognize your little investment. If you're 22 years old and you invest just $1,000, by the time you're 67, it can grow to...you won't believe this...about $73,000![7] If you don't have the $1,000 now, put $100 away per month over the next year. $1,200 invested over 45 years could top $87,000! And you didn't do a lick of work in those 45 years to make this happen. Surely, your future is worth this small investment. But you must do it now. Don't pass up your chance. The longer you wait, the less you'll have in your golden years.

If you put that same $1,000 away when you're 32, with 35 years until you retire, you would only have about $28,000. Or invest it with 25 years to go, you'd be left with about a measly $11,000. What a difference! What could you possibly buy with $1,000 now that could bring you the same benefit? Over this next year, put away $1,000 and don't touch it again. Then, go blow some money on something fun. But take care of business first.[7]

Larger investments can bring substantially larger returns. If you invest $1,000 *per year* for 10 years, then let it sit for the next 35 years, you could have over $492,000. If you wait 10 years, then do the same exercise, investing $1,000 *per year* for 10 years, let it sit for 25 years, you'd have almost $190,000, losing out on about $300,000. And, for my final example, if you invest $1,000 *per year for 45 years*, you could retire with not $45,000, but over $790,000![7]

Note that it's important that you use the correct equation. In addition to the amount you'll put away and the interest rate you'll receive, patience and faith are part of the formula. Let me explain. In the early years, the returns on your investment may feel a little scrawny. After all, 10% of $1,000 is only $100. So, after your first year of saving $1,000, if you got 10% on your money, you would have earned a whopping $100. Yaaawwwwn. Right. Not a big deal. However, if you keep putting it away, and never take out the principal or interest, keep earning that 10%, after 10 years of saving $1,000 per year (you'd have about $17,500) your annual return will be more like $1,700. That's not too shabby. But keep it up. After 20 years? Your earnings alone (not including the initial amount or cash you keep adding) would be more like $6,000 per year. Continue saving and...yada yada yada....when you're ready to retire with that $790,000 we calculated earlier...your stacks could be throwing off $79,000 per year in earnings alone. Now that's exciting. But, you have to keep it up, keep the faith, practice patience. Remember, you're securing your future.

If you are in your 20's or younger and you start to invest a little bit now, it can come back to you in unimaginable returns. If you're in your 30's, this topic applies to you more than ever. If you are in your 40's or older, you had

---

7 This is "Compound Interest" at work. I'll get into the details of this concept in Chapter Six, "Investment Briefs." In the examples in this section, a 10% per year rate of return is used. The stock market (S&P 500) has provided an annualized growth rate of approximately 10% over the last 25 years. (Data from http://www.moneychimp.com/features/market_cagr.htm, where they have a nifty historical returns calculator for the S&P 500 (S&P 500 is explained in Chapter Six, MARKET INDEX). Put in starting and ending dates and it will give you the annualized growth rate over those years.) Rates of return and interest rates can fluctuate wildly. There is no guarantee that the market will continue to return 10%, but if you go to fincalc.com (under Investment Calculators, to "The value of compound interest," as I used for these calculations), or another compound interest calculator (more are provided in Chapter Two in the I WANT IT NOW! section), you can see the results of your own examples using different investment amounts and different rates of return. It's really interesting! Even if you use a much smaller rate of return, remember that your time-benefited compounded returns will be much higher than spending your money now.

better get a move on. It's not too late, but it might be, if you don't take the information in this book to heart. No matter your age...I'm talking to you. Start now. This is absolutely one of the most important decisions you will ever make to assure your own happiness, security, and ability to reach your dreams. Don't be like so many others who are 10, 20, and 30 years older than you who don't have any security in the bank, handcuffed to their jobs, praying they don't get downsized because they didn't do what it took to be happy and secure 30, 20, or 10 years earlier. Start now.

BUSTING "BUT I JUST WANT IT"

I know you want it. I want it too. There are many, many things we want. The things we want live on a continuum—from the left end, what you want and there's no problem buying it, to the right end, what you want but you will never have because it doesn't fit into your personal economics and you are perfectly comfortable with that. The ends are easy.

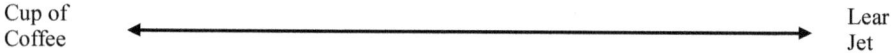

The trouble comes when purchases fall in the middle, when you don't accurately estimate where on the continuum they lie. A one-time treat may fall over to the left, "can afford it," side. But continuously buying those pleasures creeps much further to the right, "can't afford it," side. A larger one-time purchase may also sit toward the center or more firmly to the right.

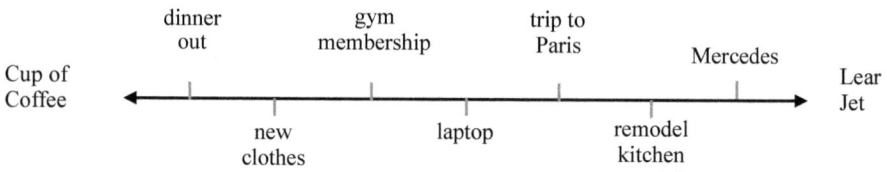

What's happening here is that the desire part of your brain has grown much larger and robust than the atrophied, logical, self-disciplined part of your brain.[8]

---

8 Full disclosure: I'm just making this up...but you get the picture.

What's Missing?

You don't want to deny yourself. You want to consume, own, experience. Maybe you feel you've denied yourself for long enough. Or, maybe you feel like a person who should "have." You are confident, have self-respect and pride. You want it. You get it.

You need to consider the gratification you feel in context with your larger spending life, your fiscal month, and your bigger goals—not just how it makes you feel, or how you think it will make you feel now.

You intellectually understand all this...but...you may still just want it. Why so badly? Is there another deeper reason why you are spending? So many people are buying things to try to make them happy, then wonder why they're not. Is something missing? Are you substituting the good feeling of that purchased comfort for something more fundamental? What is it you really want? Love? Friendship? Family? Self-respect? Relaxation? Are you over-stressed? Unemployed? Overweight? Have you experienced a loss or trauma that is still haunting you? I recognize that what I'm saying can be hard to hear and maybe even harder to admit. You need to get to the heart of the issue that you are masking and work on it.

Shopping, spending, and consuming is not the answer, even if it feels really good at the moment. It will not fill that void. In fact, it will probably make it worse. The good emotions you feel will fade shortly, and you will end up with a weaker financial future.

You've come to the first exercise in the book. Throughout these pages, exercises will be accompanied by this pen and paper graphic so you can easily identify them.

If what you read above describes you, this exercise is for you:

A. Write one thing that is missing in your life, troubling you, or making you unhappy:

B. List three things you can start to do to improve this situation.

1.

2.

3.

Repeat the above with as many issues as are troubling you.

C. For each issue, flesh out a full action plan: break down the actions you wrote under B. above and fill in details. Add further actions or particular steps to take, people you need to speak with, what you'll say, books to read, internet research to do, help or support to get, etc.

D. Take action! Do it!

I admit it. Shopping and buying feels good. It feels powerful. You feel in control, in command, decisive and dominant. These days when we refer to a powerful person, outside of holding very high political office, generally we mean they have a lot of money—and with that money they can wield a lot of influence. So how can we mere work-a-day mortals play in their league?

We need to redefine the word "powerful". Have you ever met someone who is powerfully smart? How about powerfully persuasive? Powerfully creative? What if we start using this word more broadly? "She is powerfully kind. He is powerfully generous. They are powerfully friendly."

What is your power? Recognize it. Appreciate it. Focus on what you are good at—what you are great at. Take a deep breath. Expand your chest. Put your hands on your hips. You are powerful—and it's not about money.

Hooked

Those expensive treats you give yourself are like a drug. It feels good for a while, addicting you to that feeling, but like a drug they are eroding your (financial) health.[9]

Do any of these behaviors resonate with you: you buy more than you need, spend more than you have, think about or go shopping often, feel guilty or shameful, keep shopping secrets, have money problems because of your spending or it has caused strained or uncomfortable relationships? If so, you may have a more serious problem that I encourage you to examine. Do some research on the phrases "compulsive buying disorder," "shopaholic," "shopping addiction," or the technical term, "oniomania." If you feel you may have an issue with shopping, please seek help. Find a therapist or a good friend to confide in. If you are working, ask your company if they have an EAP (employee assistance program) with free counselors you can contact. Search the Internet for online help/support groups, Debtors Anonymous and other resources.

Whether your habit is more or less serious, when you get the urge, substitute it with other activities like spending fun time with your kids, partner, or pet, exercising, calling a friend, reading, working, listening to music, making dinner, taking a walk, writing, anything else that doesn't involve a purchase.

Stop spending to feel better. Fix the underlying cause, so you can spend appropriately and stop mortgaging your future.

BUSTING "BUT IT WAS SUCH A GREAT DEAL I COULDN'T PASS IT UP"

You're in your favorite store. You see a sign. "75% OFF."

WOW! Your heart starts to beat. You head over to take a closer look. "What's 75% off? Will I like it? Does it fit? Can I use it? DOES IT MATTER?! IT'S 75% OFF!

---

9 If you often "treat" yourself, be aware that a "treat" is defined as "an event or item that is out of the ordinary and gives great pleasure." Treating yourself regularly is an oxymoron.

Are you the type whose heartbeat speeds up in the face of a really great deal? Then, when you see that today's the last day it's available, your pulse races even faster, shooting blood through your heart (which really wants you to buy it) and up and around to your head (which is raging a debate between your finances and the fantastic deal you'll never find again and how you'd be an IDIOT TO PASS IT UP!)

Whoa. Hang on. Take a breath. Is it really the deal it appears to be?

Based on a true story:

Loretta, always aware of her finances, was reading the paper when she spotted a special on her brand of cosmetics at her favorite department store:

Weekend Special

Luscious Lover Lipstick, Steamy Seduction Mascara, and Lift & Tuck Face Cream
This weekend only, get these amazing beauty basics PLUS a lovely Pink Paisley Tote

A $60 VALUE

Our gift to you, with a minimum purchase of $15.99

"What a great deal!" she thought, "I can't pass that up." So, to save money, she went down to the store to collect her "gift." To meet her minimum purchase, she picked up Smokey Joe's Auburn Eye Shadow. But when she got to the register she discovered that it only cost $14.75 (*only!*). Well, to save the money she intended to, she had to buy one more item to reach the $15.99 minimum. She picked up the cheapest thing they had in the counter: Manhunt Maroon Nail Polish for $7.50. Loretta thanked the clerk for the "free" gift and turned to leave. On her way to the door, she noticed the "CLEARANCE" rack of Spring Fashions, and headed over to take a look. Two hundred and twenty-five dollars later, Loretta realized that she had better get the heck out of that store!

Advertisements for stores from hardware to baby wear will have amazing "Super Sale" items. Sometimes the deal is so good you wonder how they can make a profit. Maybe they're not—not on that one well-publicized item. But they're making a killing on the 10 other products you've got in your arms by the time you reach the register.

Recently, Kara, a coworker, told me the story of how she went into a very expensive clothing store because of the sign in the window that touted:

"EVERYTHING ON SALE! CLEARANCE! 70% OFF!"

Normally, she would never shop there, but at sale prices like that, she could actually afford those high quality, designer garments. There were lots of beautiful clothes and some terrific discounts.

What a fun afternoon she had in her luxury dressing room trying on haute couture, sipping on a glass of wine, and being pampered by snooty saleswomen. She made her final choices and pulled out her credit card.

Her total was a lot more than she expected. When she asked about the "70% OFF," she was told, "Oh, no Madame. That is only on *blue* lined items. Your pieces are *aqua* lined, which are 30% off."

Suddenly, the deal she couldn't pass up became a trap she couldn't get out of. She invested hours in that store, she was primped and praised her in good faith and she was too attached to the clothes to put them back.

When you see amazing prices, ask yourself, "What's the trick?"

The super discounts or free bonuses retailers offer are probably either a "loss leader" (one item priced exceedingly low), or cheap, low quality, closeouts that aren't worth the material they're made with. Both are designed to lure you into the store so you will hopefully buy other, full-priced goods. Recognize the hook to get you into the store. Don't fall for the tricks. Take advantage of the good deals, but stop there.

When a store advertises a "GREAT DEAL," what it really means is, "Come on in and spend a *great deal* of your money here."

The Incredible Bulk

Those enormous bulk-buying food outlets are a fine way to save money if you are throwing a party, have a large family, or own a small business. If you are single or have a small family, chances are you may be wasting money by shopping there. It's true that you may pay much less on a per ounce basis. But, when half of the container goes bad, you would have spent more per ounce on the portion you used than its regular-sized, retail counterpart. On top of that, you pay an annual premium, and if you don't live nearby, you pay the gas or transportation cost to get there, which effectively increases the cost of every item you buy.

The extra-large containers can be hard to store and may take up too much space. Keep only what you can clearly see and will fit comfortably in your cabinets, pantry or storage. If it's hiding in your cabinets behind stacks of boxes or cans and you can't see it, you won't use it, and you'll be wasting food, money, and space.

Let's Make a Deal

Let's Make a Deal is a game show where contestants have a few mystery options to choose from:

"What's behind Curtain Number One?...

What's in the Wooden Box?...

...or...

What Carol is holding?"

They choose one; hoping they will win a valuable prize. Then, they find out if their deal was a good one:

"A brand-new washing machine! "

...or a very disappointing one:

"A live donkey and one year's supply of donkey food"

On TV, it's a funny gag, but in real life we should never be disappointed with our deals.

Not Quite Right

How would you like it if I could give you back all the money you have spent over the years on super sale items that seemed like a great addition to your life, but you never actually used? How much money would I be giving you? A few hundred dollars? A few thousand? More? Much more? Don't give in to good intentioned temptations. It is, in fact, not true what the ads say, "...the more money you spend, the more money you save." The truth is: the more money you spend, the more money you spend. And the less there is for the stuff you really need and will use.

You may find that an unbelievably inexpensive item becomes quite believable when it falls apart before it should. Suddenly it's turned around, and you feel you seriously overpaid. Before you revel in your cut-rate coup, look closer. Check the seams, joints, materials, and workmanship. We who are susceptible to bargain fever (you know the signs: sweats, shakes, uncontrollable giggling), must admit that our annoying friends and fathers can be right: "You do (sometimes) get what you pay for."

Watch out for getting swept away with a heart-stopping bargain that is not exactly what you need. If it's not perfect or you'll hardly ever use it, it will just be a disappointment and take up space in your home for months or years until you finally earn a nickel for it in a garage sale.

Tricky Charges

1. Extras: Make sure you know about all of the costs involved. Frequently, the seller will add layer upon layer of hidden charges, like installation fees, options, warranties, maintenance, finance charges, upgrades and accessories that are actually necessary to make it work.[10]

   Before you commit, ask the salesperson, "What other charges are involved?" Then, keep asking that until he says there are no more. All

---

10 Brand-new, V8, and Cherry-Red Zoomster with Dual Cams, Alloy Rims, and gorgeous Duraluxx Finish! Yours! To drive off the lot for ONLY $5,500!!! Actual prices may vary. Some restrictions apply.

Upgrades, sports package, tires, doors, windshield, windows, gas tank and engine sold separately. Taxes and license not included.

costs should be considered before you decide to buy. The cost of taxes, licenses, shipping and handling are still coming out of your pocket and can be significant, especially on higher priced items. So many extra charges give you a lot to negotiate. If they're going to be tricky, you can too. This approach works well:

To the salesperson, after she tells you about all the extras involved:

"That's so disappointing. I really wanted to buy this. I understood the entire cost to be the price that's marked. That's all I can afford. I really do want it. Are all those extras necessary? Is there anything you can do to help me out?"

And let the negotiating begin. You will likely get some price reductions.

2. Infrequent Charges: Don't consider up-front membership fees and annual dues are "one-time charges, so they don't really count," like the salespeople are trying to convince you. Try to negotiate these payments down. Add in the one-time or monthly fees to see what it's really costing you.

3. Bump Ups: "Deals" that start at a great rate then get hiked up later aren't deals. They make up the discount you got in the first few months plus more over time. Go for it only if you can and will cancel after the discount portion of the deal is done.

You Call That a Deal?

- "Buy One Get One Free": If you need two, instead of just one, this may be a deal.

- "Buy Two Get One Free": It's probably not worth it. Do you need three? Don't spend the extra.

- "Buy Three, Four, or Five, and Get One Free": How many do they think we need? This is pretty thin incentive.

That extra one isn't free. The profits you're providing on all of your excess shopping more than pays for that one additional "freebie."

- "10% off": Most retailers mark up their goods 100% from what they paid for it. A 10 percent discount is not much of a sacrifice. You call that a deal? Show me 25-50% off. Now, I'm shopping.

- "Free Drink With the Purchase of Every Dinner": Are you kidding me?

These sales devices are weak. They should do better to attract your business.

A Nasty Bargain that Bites Back:

Greg stumbles onto a heart-stopping sale on the new computer he's been coveting for months. Today only—it's 50% off. He can get a $1,000 computer for $500. No hidden costs, no tricks—it's the real deal. He puts it on his store card. Oh, happy day!

Greg then goes on with his life as normal, doing what he always does, paying the minimum monthly charges on his card. (Here comes the nasty part...)

It will take Greg almost eight years and $431 in interest before he pays it off!

The $500 computer will cost him $931.

See note for how Greg pays down his debt.[11]

When Opportunity Knocks

...you're supposed to answer. But what if Opportunity shows up at your door with 150 of his closest friends? You can't take advantage of every possibility that comes your way. That's obvious. You have to choose.

Imagine your favorite store is going out of business and I drop you down into the middle of it on its last day. The deals are outrageous. The signs say, "EVERYTHING MUST GO/MAKE AN OFFER." Here, we have Mr. Opportunity and all his pals, each one begging you to, "Choose me! Choose

---

11 $10 per month minimum payments, the credit card has an 18% interest rate. Calculation generated using, "How long will it take to pay off my credit card?" under Credit Card Calculators at www.fincalc.com.

me!" What to do? A minute ago it was obvious. But, when you're in the thick of it, it's not so clear. Answer: be strong. Choose one, if any.

Opportunity abounds in every aisle of the bulk-buying warehouse. His brothers taunt you in the factory outlets. Cousins endlessly dance across the screen of the Shop-From-Home TV Networks. And (my personal weakness) every exotic and designer beauty beckons from the shelves of countries where the dollar buys a lot more than we're used to.

Set your limits. Tell yourself, "Calm down. You are not going to be irresponsible about this. It's not a deal if you weren't going to buy it anyway. If you can afford it, choose one item. Pay cash. No credit. Be smart and stay in control."

Ask and Ye Shall Find

There are many shades of deals out there, plenty with tricks, undisclosed extras, minimum purchases, or poor quality. Then, there are a few rare gems hidden among the false goods that are real bargains—true and pure of heart. These we believe in and search for in earnest. Yet, they are all advertised the same. They all appear to be credible. How can we know which to trust?

Ask.

If there's no obvious trick or catch but the deal seems too good to be true, ask the salesperson how the company is making money off of the sale. No one works for free and no business makes a sale that doesn't benefit them. It's all about profit. It's an unspoken truth. Business owners know it, and the customers (usually) know it. Yet it is rarely, almost never, discussed.

Most people are content to puzzle over their questions, quietly wondering to themselves if the deal they're contemplating is genuine or will bite them later. If you ask, you can probably get the answers you need to make an informed decision. I've found that salespeople like to speak with people on their own level about themselves, their job, and their company. Break through the imaginary scrim of us vs. them, customer vs. corporation. More than likely, they will tell you whatever it is you want to know.

If someone wants to do work for you and not charge you—big red flag! Ask them whatever comes to mind: "How are you (or your company) being paid if you're not charging me?" Once you get into it, you may find that there's a monthly charge about which they weren't so forthcoming. Or, you may find that they are being paid elsewhere. This is often the case with brokers: travel agents are paid by the airlines; car dealers are paid extra bonuses from the manufacturers. Free Internet services are paid by companies who buy advertising space on their websites, or they are simply building up a large enough audience to sell their site and loyal following to a corporate conglomerate. In all these cases, the money isn't coming (directly) from you. There are no hidden charges, so you can relax.

> There once was a girl from Peru.
> With her money, she knew what to do.
> She never used credit.
> She said, "Just forget it!"
> And her savings account grew & it grew.

BUSTING "BUT IT'S NOT FOR ME, SO IT DOESN'T COUNT"

It's your girlfriend's birthday. You sure would like to get her something nice. You've seen her eyeing a terrific little black dress and you know she'd love it. Of course, it does cost a pretty penny—more than you probably should spend. But she's a great friend, and she deserves it. It would feel so good to make her day.

Whenever you're away from home you're keeping an eye out for a present for your friend who's watching your pet, and you really should bring something back for your coworkers. A little treat for your partner goes without saying. The next thing you know, your bags are bulging with special somethings for everyone. How much did those mementos cost? Are they in your budget? Can you afford them? "Well that really doesn't apply; these things aren't for me. I can't help it; I'm just a nice person."

What happens when holidays come around? Holiday cheer for everyone! You love your friends and family and you show them with your generosity. One present seems so scrawny. Two or three looks better. It feels so good to make people happy. After all, the phone company will understand that your January payment may be a tad late. They have friends too, don't they?

Mother's Day is right around the corner. Great. You now have the perfect opportunity to do some "destination" shopping. You leave your house with one sole purpose: to buy. True, the purchase doesn't remain with you, but the shopping experience is the same. The rush of the buy is still there. The salespeople will fawn over you like usual. You've got a gift to get, money in your pocket and you know how to spend it. You are in control. So get dressed like you mean it and grab your wallet with conviction, 'cuz you ain't coming back 'til you've got a gift to make a mother proud.

For many of us, even if we've been diligent in keeping ourselves financially in-line, and staying within our budget, when it comes time to buying gifts for friends, we give ourselves spending carte blanche. Since we love our friends and family, we want nothing more than to make them happy. And what makes someone happier than an expensive treat? Because you are such a good friend, spouse, parent, sibling, coworker, or child, you want a tangible way of showing how much you care; your generosity floweth over. After all, "Budgets don't really count, it's not for me."

Being a generous person is certainly a virtue. But it is *not*, by far, your most attractive quality. This we know because your friends and family like to spend time with you on many other occasions aside from just the gift-giving ones. They see and enjoy all of your wonderful qualities whether or not you ever spend a dime on them. That is why they want to spend their time with you on their special day. Your family and friends love you (even if they never tell you) and care about you because of who you are, not for the material things you give them.

I have to admit that the people in your life probably do want you to spend on them—but it's your time, not your coin. What they really want is you: your time, your caring, your shoulder, your ear, and your smile. If I took your friends aside and asked them to tell me the things they love about you, "The presents he/she gives me" would never appear on the list.

I know you want to be generous, but you must also be responsible. How would you feel if your good friend was sinking further into credit card hell...falling down into that never-ending spiral of minimum payments and interest fees, just to buy you a gift? What do you think your buddy would say if he knew you were spending more than you could afford, getting into debt, to buy him a birthday present? You'd probably never hear the end of it. So don't do it.

Any gift given, no matter the price, is a complete package unto itself.

It's a sincere collection of...

- the time you took thinking about your friend, and deciding what to get
- your shopping efforts
- your hard-earned money
- more of your time and creativity to wrap it up
- your search for the perfect card
- your attendance at the party

...all tied up in ribbon.

You've already given a terrific gift, and no one knows what's inside the box yet. Subconsciously, the person receiving the present is aware of all this. All the time and effort, what you went through to buy and prepare that present, is the real gift. The amount you spent is irrelevant.

Be there with them. Be in the moment. Share the day. Share your time. Expand your friendship but don't expire your bank account. It's a win-win for everyone.

And, by the way, it does count. Spending is spending is spending.

Are You An "OVER-GIFTER?"

Do you feel bad showing up with only one gift? Do you really want to make their day with a pile of prezzies? One stacked on top of the other is so much more exciting. What happens when the holidays roll around? Christmas cheer for everyone! You love your friends and family and you show them with your generosity. One present each seems so scrawny. Two or three looks much better. And then the stockings need to be stuffed. It feels so good to make people happy.

You're an Over-gifter if you:

- feel bad, guilty, or unworthy showing up with only one gift per person.

- want to be everyone's Santa, spreading joy and happiness with presents galore.

- get (further) into debt buying gifts.

- just plain spend too much on presents.

Here is the simple fact: ONE GIFT IS ENOUGH.

If you want to add the feeling of more gifts without the added spending, throw in some stocking stuffers. Make them low-priced and fun: chocolates, toys, accessories, etc. Or, add a little something to the outside of the package. Dangle an ornament or candy from the bow.

What are the holidays all about, anyway? They're about love. That's what they say in the Christmas carols. That's what the cards illustrate. The good cheer of the season comes from gathering close to those you hold special, and sharing food, stories and laughs. It's also about helping others in need and reaching out. It is only corporate commercialism (modern malls and credit card companies) that got us into these crazed, overspending, winter sprees. Have you ever heard a sermon that referred to video games and new skiing equipment? Have you ever seen a classic holy masterpiece that depicts Jesus receiving a leather jacket or a mountain bike? (Ok, it's true that there is mention of a couple of wise men coming from the east...bearing presents...but they were kings. If you own a country or run a nation, you are exempt from this point. If you are wearing a crown now, skip ahead to Chapter Three.)

Every year during the season of good tidings, you run all over tarnation, cleaning your home for guests, cooking up a storm, shopping like a madman, or packing and rushing and waiting for hours in crowded airports. Everything needs to be prepared and purchased for everyone else. It's time you got a present for yourself once a year. Give yourself the gift of good sense. Rise above the mania. Keep your own sugar plum dreams in mind. First, you'll have to determine how much you can afford to spend on everybody in total. Then, you can buy as many presents as you want for each, as long as you stay within the amount you decided on up front. With the help of the following section, "More Than You Know," you will make your own PRESENT PLAN, a complete, individualized guide to good-sense giving. Refer to the "GIFT-GIVING" section in Chapter Four for specific, inexpensive gifting ideas.

There is No Room For Guilt at the Inn

Isn't it funny the places we can find guilt? For some of us, it's everywhere: at home, at work, when we're relaxing, and there it is again waiting under the tree. What is it doing there? Guilt is ready to pounce if a friend cheats and spends more than he was supposed to on the gift exchange. It chews on you if you get an unexpected gift and have nothing in return. Don't let it in. The way other people conduct themselves and their gifting is completely up to them. If they choose to buy extravagant gifts, that's their choice. You can't control their behavior. Thank them for the gift, possibly acknowledge that they cheated, then move on.

Stop the madness. Think about the other side. Don't make your friends feel bad, cheap, or that they must reciprocate. Keep it to one simple, heartfelt gift. Wrap it up and make it look great.

You may want to make an agreement with your friends not to exchange gifts, or let them know that you aren't able to give presents this year (just do it well ahead of time, so they don't go shopping before you tell them).

More Than You Know

Do you know how many gifts you typically give within a year? Of course, there are birthdays—brothers, sisters, and good friends. Then, there's Christmas and Hanukkah. So it seems there are a few gifting occasions...

Let's really get into this and actually see, within the next year, how many ribbons you'll be curling and bows you'll be sticking. And, just for kicks, let's find out how much you'll be spending at the end of it all. Your "Present Plan" will make it clear.

You can download a clean Present Plan form at my website, MoneySmartHappyHeart.com. Some forms require a password to open. The password is "success."

Under each gifting occasion, write the names of the people you will be buying presents for. In the column "Approximate Amount You Currently Spend on Each Gift," write just that, about how much you typically spend on each gift. After you have filled in all the occasions, if you use my Present Plan from the website the total amount you spend will be totaled for you. For now, ignore the column to the right, "Amount You Can Afford to Spend on Each Gift." We will come back to that column in Chapter Three.

For each of the holidays and happy days, make sure you consider all of the below.

> **Couples:** If you are part of a couple, consult your partner to make sure you're not forgetting anyone.

Immediate family: spouse, kids, mom, dad and siblings

- Girlfriends, boyfriends

- Aunts, uncles, cousins, nieces and nephews

- Grandmothers and grandfathers (great grandparents?)

- Friends, neighbors, coworkers, bosses and employees you get presents for

- Are there any spouses, girlfriends, boyfriends, kids or relatives of any of the above you gift?

- Throw in a few contingencies, as you will inevitably be invited to birthday or other parties you don't anticipate throughout the year.

- Cub scout leaders, teachers, trainers, clergy, babysitters, coaches, postman, gardeners...all who apply.

- Add extra lines if you need to.

Below is an example of what your Present Plan will look like once it is completed. There are many more occasions on the actual spreadsheet. I have included a truncated example here to save space.

PRESENT PLAN		
	Approximate Amount You Currently Spend on Each Gift	Amount You Can Afford to Spend on Each Gift
Birthdays		
Name: Maya	$60	$
Name: Austin	$30	$
Valentine's Day		
Name: Sweet Pea	$125	$
Easter		
Name: Isabel	$30	$
Name: Lucas	$30	$
Mother's Day		
Name: Mom	$75	$
Name: Grandma	$50	$
Father's Day		
Name: Dad	$75	$
Name: Grandpa	$50	$
...more occasions are listed on the actual form.		
Totals	$525	$

Who knew there were so many presents to buy? Did you have any idea you were so generous? I have just been shining a light deep into the abyss of one of our blackest holes of cash, one of those Twilight Zones where money mysteriously vaporizes, and at the end of the month, we have, "...no idea where it could have gone."

To make your Present Plan, you will decide how much you *can* spend on *all* presents, for everyone during the entire year, then divide that amount out for each person and each gift. You don't need to decide what you will get them now, and you can shift the amounts between people and gifts as the year progresses. Although, it would be difficult to know exactly how much you can really afford to spend on gifts without giving thought to the rest of your monthly bills. (You can't buy presents for the little league coach, when you can't pay the gas bill.) In Chapter Three, you will consider how much money you bring home, how much you must spend to pay your basics and how much you can afford to spend on other people's wish lists. Then, you'll come back to this section and use that third column to finalize your Present Plan.

Speaking of wishes, let's do some dreaming...

Chapter 2

DO SOME DREAMING

PERSONAL EVALUATION: Life Fundamentals

Have you ever created a personal strategic plan? This is the process of putting a pin in the map of your life, so you know what direction to head. Once this is done, you can ignore the noise that is so often present and listen only to the music that is calling you in the right direction. Your direction. You can follow the route that will lead you to who you really want to be, who you really are. The exercises below will help you unfold the map, find your location, then stay on course.

This book takes a holistic approach to your financial life. These exercises will help focus your energy on feeling happier and more satisfied, and as you will see at the end of this section, they also directly relate to increasing your wealth.

> **Couples:** Complete the following five exercises below separately, then share your answers. Not only will they help you align and focus your spending, they will help you understand each other more fully. You will gain a deeper appreciation for each other and uncover opportunities to support one another in your pursuit for a successful financial life and to generally find more fulfillment and satisfaction individually and together.

FOR YOUR LIFE

What do you want *for* your life? How do you want to feel? We all want to be rich. But why? What would you do with it? You would use it to achieve something, ultimately a state of mind or a feeling. Let's see an example. If I had a million bucks, I'd quit my job and I'd buy a boat. Why? So I can get out in the sun and spend hours sailing. Why? So I can feel happy, alive, relaxed and free. This is what it comes down to. This is bigger than the big picture; these are your ultimate goals. We are all striving to attain a certain emotional state. What are you working toward? Your list may include some of the following:

I'd like to be happy.

I'd like to be healthy.

I'd like to have more energy.

I'd like to be more confident.

I'd like to feel:

- accepted and a part of a group
- less stressed
- proud
- safe & secure

If you could buy anything at all, what would it be...and why? It is to achieve these goals. Maybe you'd buy an island. Why? So you could lie around on it. Why? To be relaxed, centered, not rushed, and not always responding to someone else's orders, to feel happy and proud, to share your island with your friends so you could spend more time with them, your family or by yourself.

Take a few minutes and write down your own list below. Answer the question, **"What do you want FOR your life?"** These are your ultimate goals—how you want to feel. Write down as many as you can think of.

There is a section for this on the Personal Evaluation form at my website MoneySmartHappyHeart.com. Some forms require a password to open. The password is "success."

THE SECRET SAUCE OF HAPPINESS

Everyone wants money. Almost everyone wants *more* money. But how much fun is lying in a room full of money? What everyone actually wants is to be happy, and money buys us the stuff that will make us happy. At least, that's what we think. How close is that connection, really? In order to find out, we need to understand happiness. What is it? Where do we find it? How much does it cost? What's the secret sauce?

The happiness I am referring to is deeper than the momentary pleasures that are fun or feel good only while you are experiencing them. Digging into a decadent, fudgy, chocolate cake is heaven—for a short time. We have all experienced that first scrumptious bite that shoots off little flavor fireworks in our mouths. The second bite is not quite as good as the first, and then each subsequent bite delivers less and less pleasure. "Pleasure" gives you temporary fun, excitement, exhilaration, or enjoyment. The "happiness" we pursue is more essential, fulfilling, and lasting. It's an overarching sense of well-being, a satisfaction with life, a feeling in your core that just makes you want to smile.

Curious whether money can buy this happiness, I embarked on a journey into the research. I read books and articles and reviewed the studies. I watched TED Talks and scoured websites. I talked to counselors, coaches and engaged in guided meditations. I listened to teaching talks, joined blogs and watched films. As I expanded my exploration, I started noticing patterns; the conclusions started to overlap.

I have taken all of this material and consolidated it into simple language and actionable basics and have presented it in a straightforward, easy-to-understand format below. It's designed for you to comprehend readily and put into action immediately, if you choose to. There are full subject disciplines emerging around many of the individual aspects I have identified. You can read entire books and delve into the depths of each. My list below, although maybe not all-encompassing, contains the elements of happiness that appeared most frequently.

As I was synthesizing the data, I realized that it all fits nicely into these four very concise categories:

1. Who
2. Do
3. Woo-Hoo!
4. You

A bit more broadly, they are:

1. Who to hang with
2. What to do
3. How to think
4. How to treat yourself

The answer to each of these, simply put, is:

1. Be with your people.
2. Do what you love and give back.
3. Choose happiness and gratitude.
4. Love yourself.

In the chart below, under each of these categories, I have listed what the research says it takes to be happy. Rate yourself on how well you are adopting each element into your life.

Use a rating scale, from 1 to 10:

1 = "I pretty much suck at this."

10 = "You know, I'm all about that."

The Secret Sauce of Happiness interactive form is available at MoneySmartHappyHeart.com. Some forms require a password to open. The password is "success."

The Secret Sauce of Happiness		Rating 1-10
1. WHO: Be with your people.		
Find people and groups where you feel you belong.		
Be with others who like, accept and support you.		
Spend more time with happy people and less time with those that bring you down.		
Have in-person connections...		
...and when you do, engage in deep, meaningful conversation.		
	Section 1 score	
	points possible	50
2. DO: Do what you love and give.		
Do the things you enjoy. Lose track of time doing fun, engaging work and hobbies.		
Challenge yourself: Learn. Discover. Problem-solve.		
Have a purpose. Do work that matters and has meaning to you. (Save the world, if that excites you.)		
Have a goal. (Schedule big and little things to look forward to.)		
Focus on others. Give your time, money, and ear. (Stop concentrating on yourself and volunteer, donate, or listen to those who need it.)		

More activities that make us happy:		
Be active and sporty. Exercise.		
Be in nature.		
Listen to good music.		
Get enough sleep.		
Laugh.		
Relax.		
Develop your spirituality. (Through religion, yoga, meditating, mindfulness, etc.)		
Engage in experiences over having things.		
	Section 2 score	
	points possible	130
3. WOO-HOO!: Choose happiness and gratitude.		
Try, choose, decide to be happy.		
Always look on the bright side.		
Celebrate big and small victories.		
Appreciate simple pleasures.		
Be thankful; practice gratitude.		
Be resilient; bounce back from failure. (...and equip yourself with tools to deal with the hard times in life.)		
Live in the moment.		
	Section 3 score	
	points possible	70
4. YOU: Love yourself.		
Be yourself; be genuine. This also means be vulnerable.		
Appreciate and respect yourself.		
Have confidence.		
Don't compare yourself to others.		

Treat yourself like you would treat someone you love. (...that is, be kind to yourself; don't be too hard on yourself.)		
	Section 4 score	
	possible points	50
	Sections 1- 4 Total Score	
	points possible	300

Your Results

Add up your scores for the statements in each section, and then total all four sections onto the Section 1-4 Total Score line on the bottom. How did you do? Great job on those you scored a 7, 8, 9, or 10! You are naturally doing things that create happiness. These are your underpinnings of contentment. Now, let's build from there. On which did you score a 4, 5, or 6? You can do better. Give these areas some attention and really concentrate on the statements you gave yourself a 1, 2, or 3.

The Take Away

What do you notice about the cost of happiness? Having so little money that you can't take care of yourself or your family can cause a great deal of stress and tension in relationships; however, after having enough to afford the basics, money is not in the equation. Spending like a prince is never a factor in any of the studies, writing or advice I've come across that deal with what makes us happy.

According to Martin Seligman, the man considered the founder of the study of happiness called "positive psychology" and author of *Authentic Happiness, Learned Optimism,* and others, in his 2004 TED talk, "It turns out the pursuit of pleasure has almost no contribution to life satisfaction. The pursuit of meaning is the strongest. The pursuit of engagement is also very strong. Where pleasure matters is if you have both engagement and you have meaning, then pleasure's the whipped cream and the cherry."

Even governments are getting the message. The World Happiness Report is a new survey conducted by the United Nations that has taken place three times since 2012. It is a new way of approaching the search for improving peoples' lives. As opposed to using an economic measure, like household income or GDP (gross domestic product) to analyze and compare countries, this survey measures the well-being of the people of the world. The intention is to then use this "happiness data" to establish policies that will help people live better. Per the Report, "This new form of cost-benefit analysis avoids many of the serious problems with existing methods, where money is the measure of benefit."[12]

Do you ever experience 1% envy? I would be lying if I said I didn't. That begs the question, "Are the rich happier than the rest of us?" Studies and research show conflicting results and as I mentioned before, there is a baseline of income needed to pay for food, shelter and clothing, but once we have that covered, how much more happiness do all of their pleasures bring them? What rich people do you know of who have killed themselves or have died early because of something terrible in their lives like a drug addiction, depression, crushing shame, or a personal dispute? The wealthy worry about money, too. They have businesses that are one deal away from the end, they are concerned that their heirs will waste the money they worked so hard for, they have pressure from family and friends, and some are even living paycheck to paycheck because they are spending above their already super lavish means. Our affluent friends have ruined relationships with their spouses and children because they were too busy working to pay attention to them, and they experience any number of domestic issues that afflict them as they do us. They may not have good friends and never know whether someone is interested in them or their cash. They have fights with their loved ones, get diseases, and have failures like all of us. I am not saying that all rich people have these issues all of the time, or even some of the time. I just wanted to remind you that they are people, like us. Spending is not what makes them, or us, happy.

Tal Ben-Shaham taught the most popular course in Harvard's history. It was on the study of happiness. He said, "The core lesson seems to be that happiness comes from within and can be achieved by a shift in attitude and

---

12 http://worldhappiness.report

behavior."[13] On the popularity of his Harvard class he jokingly said, "The biggest course before that was an introduction to economics, so it's more important for people to be happy than rich."

Christopher Peterson, author, professor of psychology at University of Michigan and one of the founders of positive psychology, summed it up this way, "Happiness is a product of our pursuits. Other people matter. Anything that builds relationships between and among people is going to make you happy. Have a sense of meaning and purpose about your life. See yourself connected to something larger than yourself. People are looking for shortcuts. You have to work at it."

Make More Sauce

In this chapter I have given you the recipe for the secret sauce of happiness. Now, let's make some. Pick at least five things from the list above in which you scored a six or less. What can you do to start or increase the frequency of those elements? Commit to these actions, thoughts, or attitudes. Who needs to be involved? How often will you do it? Schedule it in your calendar.

I have provided room for this on the bottom of The Secret Sauce of Happiness form, available at MoneySmartHappyHeart.com. The password is "success."

As you fold more of the happiness factors into your life, you should start feeling lighter, less serious, more satisfied. You may find yourself smiling more often. The chorus to Pharrell Williams' "Happy" may inexplicably start

---

13 From the article: "Positive psychology has one message: be happy"

http://www.bdlive.co.za/business/management/2015/03/25/positive-psychology-has-one-message-be-happy playing in your head.[14]

So you see, the secret sauce of happiness is made up of ingredients that are readily available and are mostly all free. Strive for a life of happiness and by all means add a heaping measure of pleasure. And the good news continues: many wonderful pleasures in life are also free or low-cost. Chapter Four will help you find them. Incorporate the elements of happiness into your life. Put your credit card away and smother yourself with a generous topping of delicious happiness sauce.

WHO TO BE

In this section you will answer two questions:

Who do you want to be?

What do you want to accomplish?

Basically, you are envisioning what you want to be remembered for. You are finishing this sentence: "At the end of your life you will be at peace with yourself because you were a person who..." Be as specific as possible. Consider yourself, family, work and community. Here's an example:

I want to be a great husband.

I want a happy marriage.

I want to raise happy and healthy children.

I want to make the world a better place by caring for the environment.

---

14 "Because I'm happy - Clap along if you feel like a room without a roof - Because I'm happy - Clap along if you feel like happiness is the truth - Because I'm happy - Clap along if you know what happiness is to you - Because I'm happy - Clap along if you feel like that's what you wanna do": chorus to Pharrell Williams' Happy.

I want to be a manager in the marketing department of a multinational corporation.

I want to travel to three countries in the next seven years.

I want to give back to my community by volunteering to help the elderly.

There are so many things we can do with our time, energy, and money. Without goals, we can become scattered, confused, and never really achieve anything. By answering these questions, our guiding star comes clearly into view and we know what to accept in our lives and what to let fall by the wayside.

Answer these questions:

1. Who do you want to be?

2. What do you want to accomplish?

Your goals may change over time as opportunities open up and priorities shift. You can come back and revisit these questions periodically.

You can use the Personal Evaluation form at my website at MoneySmartHappyHeart.com. Some forms require a password to open. The password is "success."

WHAT TO DO

Let's talk about your time. If you could do anything, if you had that million bucks and didn't have to work, what would you do? What would make you go to sleep at night feeling you had a good, worthwhile, fulfilling day? This is why we do what we have to do, to be able to do what we want to do. Here's an example of what someone may want to do with his time:

I'd spend time with my family and friends.

I'd have more time for myself, to relax and enjoy my life.

I'd read more.

I'd spend more time on my favorite hobby.

I'd volunteer and help people.

I'd hike.

I'd learn to speak French.

I'd travel.

I'd learn to play the guitar.

I'd write.

Answer the question "What would you do with your time?" Prioritize as you write your list. Put what you desire to do the most at the top of the list, and continue down in order.

You can use the Personal Evaluation form at my website, MoneySmartHappyHeart.com. Some forms require a password to open. The password is "success."

WHO'S IT FOR

Now, one last exercise to examine your life. This one is a bit pointed and may give you pause, but for some people, it has so much influence over what they do with their time, energy, and money. This one doesn't need much explanation:

Who are you trying to impress?

It's a singular question, but may have many answers. Write your list with pure honesty and without thinking about it too much. Some people might be trying to impress their:

- father, mother
- brother, sister
- coworkers, boss

- best friend
- girlfriend, boyfriend
- old college roommate
- child's teacher

You can use the Personal Evaluation form at my website, MoneySmartHappyHeart.com. Some forms require a password to open. The password is "success."

So, who are you trying to impress? And why? What are you doing to that end? How much are you spending? Do you really need to? It's prudent to impress your boss and your spouse, but I'm digging deeper to uncover unhealthy insecurities that lead to damaging behaviors. Think about each person you identified and their foibles, their self-doubt. Do you think they are exerting their energy to impress you? Where can you back off, care less, spend less, and be more genuinely yourself?

THE FOUNDATION

Look at the lists you just created. This is what makes you tick! This is who you are and where you are headed. How close are you to having your ultimate life? What steps can you take right now to get you closer?

The exercises and information in this chapter provide the fundamentals of a satisfying, heart-happy life. You now have the foundation for a fun, fulfilling, worthwhile life, unique to you. Do you see how money and the transient pleasures money can buy barely register? When you start to feel you're getting off-track or you're tempted to buy yourself some happiness, revisit your lists and the research on happiness and find the joy you don't have to pay for.

That said, one or more of your important foundational desires may require a financial investment. That's fine. That means it's an important goal for you. Add it to the list of dreams you will create in the exercise below under DREAMS *CAN* COME TRUE. If an important foundational item requires an ongoing cost, instead of a one-time investment, make sure it's a priority in your Personal Spending Plan that you will complete in Chapter Three.

Although a few items on your list may have a cost associated with them, I am willing to bet that most do not, unless the ultimate state of mind you are working toward is, "To feel power and revenge by making all who look upon me envious of my extravagant lifestyle and all the money I throw in their faces! Ha! Ha! Ha!" (If that is one of your goals, uh, you may have some other issues to work on outside the scope of this book).

I know one feeling you are definitely not trying to achieve: stress. When you get wound up about money, your stomach knots, your chest tightens and your breathing gets shallow. Money is one of the top stressors for Americans. It puts a wedge in relationships and degrades your health. But it doesn't have to control you. You are taking charge of your situation, getting organized and learning what it takes to breathe free.

> **Couples:** Now that you have separately completed these exercises, come back together and share your answers. How can you support each other in your pursuits of a fun, happy, fulfilling life both individually and together? How can you balance your spending—of time, energy and money—so you are finding the happiness money can't buy—and saving for the big things it can?

You can feel abundant joy and well-being on any budget that is large enough to cover your basics. Then, you can invest the money you're no longer misspending trying to make yourself happy, to make your big dreams come true.

DREAMS *CAN* COME TRUE

Now, let's spend some cash—real money, not a couple hundred, but thousands. What would you buy? What do you really want? Think big. Do you want a house? A new car? Would you remodel your kitchen, or buy a cabin in the mountains? This is the easiest question you'll ever be asked. What do you want? Be selfish. Want to travel to the Italian Riviera or to Portugal's south beaches? Now don't get Fantasy Island on me. We all may want a castle in the hills with a staff of 20, or a Lamborghini, but I mean for you to identify desires that are reasonable for your life. I'm talking about the kind of dreams money can buy.

I've got a check here with your name on it. It's for a bunch of money. I am going to give it to you, and I want you to get rid of it. There's just one caveat.

You cannot spend less then $5,000. That means no fancy dinners, concerts, or weekend getaways, no new clothes, shoes, video games, or jewelry. You've got to spend it like you mean it. What do you want in a big way?

Your most coveted desires may not come in the form of material items. You may like to pay off all your credit cards, and have some money in the bank so you can feel financially secure. Do you need money to put your kids through school or pay for a wedding someday? Maybe you crave financial peace of mind. Are you entrepreneurially minded? Would you like to start a business? Or be able to leave your job and start a whole new career? Don't forget about retirement—enjoying your sunset years in comfort and style. What are your dreams?

Write down your top five dreams that money can buy and approximately how much each costs.

Although it may be fun to think about fulfilling your dreams, this is not just a game. This list has real purpose. Take your time and think about what you really want in the next 5, 10, 20, 30, or more years. Write your financial dreams down, then arrange them in order of importance. You may be able to rip off 10 or more. If you do, prioritize, and come up with your top 5. Once you have them identified, indicate next to each its approximate cost.

Couples: If you are married or have a partner, it is time to talk this over with your other half. If you are collaborating on this and you both can't agree on the same goals or on the same priority, jot down two separate lists, then work to come to a consensus over time.

I have provided a table where you can record your goals at the bottom of the Personal Evaluation form, available for download at my website, MoneySmartHappyHeart.com. Some forms require a password to open. The password is "success."

Are you sure about the priority? If not, reevaluate until they're in the right order.

There they are! Your dreams! Now, they are real. Now, they are no longer half-conscious ideas, floating around in your head, coming out only when you see someone else with these treasures. You want them. You DESERVE them. Read them to yourself. Read, "I want ——." Say it out loud. "I WANT ------!" "I DESERVE -----!"

You know what they say about dreams? They can come true.

Why Is It So Important to Identify Your Dreams?

Without these dreams, these goals, we have no sense of working toward something. Think about what you've accomplished in your life. Have you earned a degree? Ran a marathon? Lost 10 pounds? Won a contest? What have you accomplished that you were proud of? How were you able to achieve these things? They certainly weren't easy. You had a goal in mind each time.

If you can keep the big picture in mind, and work toward an identified goal, you can reach it. That's how you could pass up those scrumptious chocolate chip cookies and cheeseburgers on your diet. You had a goal; you knew if you stuck to it, you'd succeed. Saving is the same thing.

Doesn't it feel good to know that you have the power within yourself to stick to something and make it happen? This is a feeling that no amount of free wheeling spending can buy for you. This is the feeling of self-assurance and confidence, and yes, even inner-peace.

Many of us have never thought of savings in this way before, in terms of goals. Perhaps that's why we've been flailing around, wishing we could stash away some cash for later, but never really able to make it happen.

DREAM CARD

Cut out a piece of 2" x 3" hard, preferably brightly colored paper. Draw or cut out a picture that represents your #1 dream and attach it onto this card. Laminate this card if you can (or cover it back and front with invisible packing tape—frugal lamination). This will become your saving mantra.

Keep this card in your wallet with your money and credit cards. Not mixed in with your driver's license, over by your gym club membership or tucked away in some leathery fold. We want that reminder right in there with our cash, rubbing up against our dollar bills, keeping us aware of what it is we really want. Make four of these "Dream Cards." Keep one in with your cash, one in your checkbook, one with your credit cards (if you're still carrying any—we'll talk about that later) and tape one right up on your bathroom mirror, so you look at it at the beginning of every day.

These reminders will give you strength. Now, you will not forget the big picture, the reason you are working, what you really want and what you really deserve. You are halfway there. You have recognized what you want, and you are ready to go get it.

I WANT IT NOW!

Now that you know your goals and how much you'll need to attain them, we can bring it home by determining when you will be able to live your dreams. Think about your number one dream. When do you want it? I know you want it now. But you'll have to take a little shot of reality here. When do you think you'll be ready for your purchase? If you want it as soon as possible, choose a time period. Let's say 5 or 10 years. For the simplest calculation of how much per month you need to save, take how much it costs (if it's a home you want, take the amount of the down payment) and divide by your time period, 5 or 10 years, then divide that by 12 months in the year.

Saving for a Down Payment	
Amount needed	$50,000
How long to save	÷10 years
Amount to save each year	$5,000
12 months in a year	÷ 12 months
Amount to save every month	$417 per month

Mattress Mathematics

This calculation will tell you how much you need to save per month if you keep your money under your mattress. To find a more accurate picture of how much you need to save every month if you are investing your money and it is growing, we must consider the effects of "Compound Interest." Explained below.

Smart savers invest their money as they save. They earn interest, dividends and/or the value of their investment will increase, so their investment will be growing. "Compound Interest" is simply the concept of receiving interest on money invested, reinvesting the interest you just made, and receiving interest on that money, too. Interest on your interest. And, every month that you keep doing this (and continue to invest the regular monthly amount as well), it increases and increases. This is called "compounding" and it gives your savings a huge boost. (See Chapter Six "Investment Briefs" for more info on this concept.) Because of the compounding effect, you can invest less on a monthly basis (less than the simple Mattress Mathematics calculation), and still reach your goals. There is no guarantee that your money will increase in value, or that you will receive dividends or interest, especially if you invest in very risky securities, but over the long run the stock market has increased in value and many people find this is the best way to grow their money.

So, when will you have the money for your top goal? You can work with a financial planner, CPA or other knowledgeable financial expert, or for a good estimate, use one of these financial calculators on the web. They are very easy to use. You input the amounts, hit a button and they give you the answer. There are many out there. Here are some you can use:

- fincalc.com: under "Savings Calculators"

- bankrate.com: click on Calculators, then "Savings Calculators"

- fool.com: search for "calculators," click "Foolish Calculators," scroll down to "Savings"

- thecalculatorsite.com: under Financial Calculators

To understand how long it will take to save enough for your top goal, enter this information into an online calculator::

- How much you're saving for.

- How much you have saved now. (That might be $0, but some calculators need an input of at least $1.)

- How many years until you need the money. (Use an estimate here or how long you hope it might take. You'll refine this timing in the next section.)

- The interest rate you expect to receive. If you can't estimate the interest rate:

  - ask a financial advisor or investment professional, or

  - try different returns, for example 3%-7%

  - just be sure to follow through and get your money invested and working for you!

You might have just estimated that it will take you 10, 15, or more years before you can be cookin' in your own kitchen. Does that seem like a long time? Don't despair. Remember something you did 10 or more years ago? Seems like only yesterday, right? The future is right around the corner. If you had started saving 10 or 15 years ago, you'd be a lot closer to writing the check. However, if the future makes you feel overwhelmed or intimidated, just think...

Where will you be in 10 years or more if you don't start now?

We save day by day.
It's what you do today that counts.
Set your goals, then don't worry about the future.
It's what you do today that counts!

PERSONAL SAVINGS PLAN

Above we have been working on achieving one goal. Yet, a few pages earlier you identified several. Can you achieve them all? Your Personal Savings Plan is the road map to your dreams. Find out how much you need to save monthly, for each goal separately, using an appropriate time period for each. Then, add all your monthly savings amounts together. You will end up with a timetable of savings goals that will decrease as you attain each of them. As you achieve each of your objectives, you will no longer need to save for them and they will drop off the chart. To fill out your chart, follow the same steps you did for your top savings goal above. Get the amount you'll need to save each month by asking a financial expert or going to a calculator site. Enter the information: how much you're saving for, how much you have saved now, how many years until you'll need the money and the interest rate you expect to receive. The calculator will tell you how much you need to save and for how many months. Enter into your Personal Savings Plan in the cells beneath each goal, how much you'll need to save monthly for each goal.

Now that you know how much you need to put away every month, you can step back and evaluate. Will you actually be able to save this amount? Is it realistic? If you're not sure, Chapter Three will help you find out (and the rest of the book will help you make it happen). If, based on your income and your necessary spending, you know that you can't save that amount every month, rework the calculation until it is reasonable. Use longer periods of time until you reach your goal or lower the future amount needed.

See the Personal Savings Plan example below. Notice that each row represents how much you need to save *each month* over a *full year*. The amount you need to save *each year* is 12 times the amount in each cell. This was done to conserve space on the chart; otherwise, this chart would be 180 rows long. Likewise, the last row contains years 15-35; (the $297 of retirement savings each month continues for 30 years).

PERSONAL SAVINGS PLAN EXAMPLE

	Priority #1	Priority #2	Priority #3	Priority #4	Priority #5	
YEARS	Road Bike	Retirement	College Tuition	House Down Payment	Trip to Europe	**Total Monthly Savings Needed**
Multiple the amounts in each row by 12 to get annual savings needed achieve each goal	**Cost**	**Cost**	**Cost**	**Cost**	**Cost**	
	$1,500	$500,000	$35,000	$50,000	$5,000	Multiple the amounts in each cell below by 12 to get annual savings needed to achieve all of your goals
	Amount you have now toward goal	Amount you have now toward goal	Amount you have now toward goal	Amount you have now toward goal	Amount you have now toward goal	
	$100	$17,000	$4,000	$5,000	$0	
Amount to Save **EACH MONTH**:						**Totals**
1	$56	$297	$88	$231	$69	$741
2	$56	$297	$88	$231	$69	$741
3		$297	$88	$231	$69	$685
4		$297	$88	$231	$69	$685
5		$297	$88	$231	$69	$685
6		$297	$88	$231		$616
7		$297	$88	$231		$616
8		$297	$88	$231		$616
9		$297	$88	$231		$616
10		$297	$88	$231		$616
11		$297	$88			$385
12		$297	$88			$385
13		$297	$88			$385
14		$297	$88			$385
15-35		$297				$297
Interest / rate of return used for above calculations:						
	4.00%	7.00%	7.00%	7.00%	7.00%	

All monthly amounts are rounded to the nearest dollar. Online calculators may consider different assumptions, like the increase in the cost of living or the effects of taxes. To keep things simple, such complicating factors are not included in these calculations.

Calculations generated using bankrate.com → Calculators → Savings → Simple Savings Calculator

Try different combinations of goals, time periods, monthly savings, etc.

Find a blank Personal Savings Plan form at my website, MoneySmartHappyHeart.com. Some forms require a password to open. The password is "success."

THE GOLDEN YEARS

We need to talk briefly about retirement.

You are one of two types of people: a planner or the spontaneous type. Personally, I'm a planner. I like to look at my calendar and see my plans scheduled out over the next few weeks and months. I have a close friend who never carries a calendar and never makes a plan unless he absolutely has to. This way he is open and available at a moment's notice to accept last minute invitations and enjoy his day according to the situation, weather, or opportunities at hand. He enjoys each day as it comes.

Neither is right. Neither is wrong.

If you're the planning type, you've already got this covered. You spend time thinking about, analyzing and anticipating your coming days, weeks, and years. You may have already mapped out your education, your career, and your family. You've got season tickets, and you know where you're going on your next vacation. But what about retirement? Done any planning here?

If you're Mr./Ms. Get-Up-And-Go, you live in the moment and wake up to face the challenges and glories each new sunrise brings. But what about retirement? It may seem like a long way off, but one day you will be waking up and facing a whole new way of life where making money is not your main objective. Have you given any thought to this day?

What *about* retirement? Whether you've only got a few, or 40 years, to go, one thing is for sure...it's closer than you think. Remember something that happened 5 years ago? 10 years ago? Even 20 years ago? Do you ever feel like it happened "only yesterday?" Things sneak up on us. One day you will not be working. One day you will walk more slowly. You will tell stories that start with "In my day..." And you will be much, much less stressed.

Unless...

...you don't have the money you need to live.

This is not a fun thought. Most of us just choose not to go there. If you aren't on track for a comfortable, or even livable retirement, you're not alone. The National Institute on Retirement Security recently published the research report, *The Retirement Savings Crisis: Is it Worse Than We Think?* using data from a Federal Reserve survey of respondents ages 25-64 across America (nirsonline.org). They found that:

- The median retirement account balance *for all* working-age households is $3,000.

- The median retirement account balance *for near-retirement* households (ages 55-64) is $12,000.

- 67% of working households age 55-64 with at least one earner have retirement savings less than one times their annual income (which is far below what they will need to maintain their standard of living in retirement).

- 45% (38 million working-age households) do not have any retirement account savings.

- With limited retirement plan access and minimal retirement savings, the majority of American households will not be able to maintain their standard of living after retirement, even if they work until age 67.

Yikes! Not a happy picture.

They also found that *only half* of private sector employees have access to workplace retirement benefits—the lowest share since 1979! This means it's up to us, folks, to take control of our money, our spending and our retirement savings.

But hang on. Unclench your jaw. Unknot your stomach. That is a picture of the broader "them."

That isn't about you.

This is about you:

Fade in:

There's a loud happy party going on. There's a large cake with the word "CONGRATULATIONS!" on it. And there's a very content and blissful older person in the center of all the attention. It's you.

Fade out.

Cut to:

The next day you are alone in your modest house, cleaning up the cake plates from your retirement party. What do you look like? Gained a few pounds? Maybe lost a few? Your face is wrinkled from your wonderful years of life. What do your hands look like? What are you wearing?

You finish up with the dishes and feel a bit tired so you sit down on the couch. You're lost in the thoughts of your new life. A life without alarm clocks, time clocks, or lunch breaks. Now, your whole life is a lunch break. You are thinking about how you will support yourself (and maybe your spouse), when...

WHOOSH! In a bright flash, a younger person suddenly appears in the room right in front of you. It's you...from right now. You are wearing what you've got on now, and look just as surprised as the older you. You both stare at each other for a minute. The older you speaks first.

What will the older you say to the current you? Are you mad at you? Do you cock back a weary arm and try to slug the selfish, immediate-gratification, free-spending, non-saving you? The older you is scared and sad. Listen to what the older you is saying.

"I am here! Social Security isn't enough! I still have 25 years to live, and I need your help. Don't turn your back on me. Start planning now. NOW. I don't want to keep working, but I need to survive. Start saving at least 10% of your income every year for the day you won't be working, so I can enjoy my years. Do it for me. Do it for you!"

You wake up with a jolt. You look in the mirror. It was just a dream. A very bad dream. You still have time to make sure that particular dream does not come true. But the longer you wait, the worse off you'll be come that retirement party. Take the steps you need this week to start systematically saving 10%, or more of your paycheck.

Tonight when you go to sleep, you'll have another dream. You'll visit the older you again. But this time older you looks a bit more vibrant. You've got less gray and wrinkles from worrying about your finances. When the older you sees the current you, you give yourself a great big hug, thank yourself profusely for your foresight and intellect, and you take you out to breakfast to celebrate.

You've made sure that your older years really are golden.

Now that you know what has to be done, let's look at how to do it and how to avoid avoiding it...

Chapter 3

FINDING YOUR STARTING PLACE

Before we get started, I wonder if I can ask for your help. My friend Joe is planning to take a trip and he needs some assistance. He knows where he wants to go, but he doesn't exactly know how to get there. He's going to the French Polynesian island of Bora Bora and he needs directions. To help him, you need to know where he's starting from. Well, I can tell you that he lives... on the Earth. Can you give him the *precise path* he needs to take to get to where he's going?

Impossible?

I know.

How can anyone get somewhere if they don't know where they are starting from? That goes for almost anything in life—taking a trip, getting a job, or creating your financial future. So if I'm Joe, I need to look around and determine what state I'm in, what town, neighborhood, street, and house I'm in. When I know the starting point, and my destination, I can draw a line between the two—the path to take to get there. It might take him a while before he's walking in the sand, but boy, it's gonna be gooooood when he gets there.

Financially, if Joe knows where he wants to go, let's say he wants to be worth $1,000,000 when he retires, but he doesn't really know what he's got now, he can only guess how to get there. He can save money here and there, reduce his debt when he can and increase it when he needs to. This way will never work. But, if he knows exactly what his starting place is, he can connect the dots to his destination with a plan he can follow to get precisely where he wants. To determine his starting place, Joe needs to know how much current savings and other belongings of value he owns and the balance of all his credit and debt. The difference between what he *owns* minus what he *owes* is his NET WORTH.

See Joe's starting place, or Net Worth on the following page.

JOE'S NET WORTH

ASSETS What Joe Owns		Description	Average Annual Returns / Interest	Amount
Cash:	Not in a Bank or Investments	In sock drawer	0%	$80
Account Balances:	Checking	Moneytown Bank	0%	$700
	Savings	Moneytown Bank	1%	$3,250
	Money Market	Big Bucks Investment House	2%	$6,000
	Retirement Savings	401(k) @ Work	8%	$12,000
	Retirement Savings	IRA @ Moneytown	7.50%	$2,200
Other Investments:				
	Stock, Mutual Funds, Bonds, T-Bills	Mutual Fund @ Big Bucks	9%	$2,800
Real Estate:	Market Value of Home	Condo	Appreciates ~3%/yr	$125,000
Vehicles:	Market Value if he sold it	Truck	NA	$1,500
Money He is Owed:	IOU	From Sister	0%	$400
	Taxes	State Tax Refund	0%	$235
Other Valuables: (Market Value)				
	Furniture	Couch, table, chairs, bed	NA	$1,700
	Equipment	Large tools & ceramic kiln	NA	$500

Joe's Total Assets $156,365

DEBT What Joe Owes		Description	Ave Interest / Return Rate	Amount
Real Estate:	Remaining Mortgage	Condo	4.50%	$92,000
Vehicle Loans/Leases:				
	Loan Balance	Truck	8.75%	$250
Other Loans / Leases:				
	Balance	Student Loan - Homestate U.	6.50%	$1,500
Credit Cards:				
	Major Card #1	Vista	15%	$3,800
	Major Card #2	Discolor Card	13%	$4,375
	Store Card	Stellar Electronics Inc.	19.50%	$2,600
Other Joe Owes: Taxes, Loans, Settlements, etc.		Federal Income Tax	0%	$425

Joe's Total Debt $104,950

Joe's Net Worth $51,415
His Total Assets Minus His Total Debt

Pretty normal stuff. He's got some assets and some debt. Joe's Net Worth is positive; he's got more belongings than debt. That's a good thing. His starting place is $51,415. But how does he go from here to the $1,000,000 he wants? First he's got to get his debt down. We'll concentrate on all of his debt except his mortgage. (Since owning your own home is a dream for most people and as there is virtually no other way to own a home than to carry a mortgage, plus a tax deduction comes along with the interest on the loan, we put the mortgage payment aside.)

FROM JOE TO $1,000,000 IN SIX PARAGRAPHS

There are only two simple parts to the strategy: reduce debt, then create and follow a reasonable savings and investing plan.

Reduce Debt:

1. Aside from his mortgage, and after he pays his income taxes, Joe needs to reduce his debt—those with the highest interest rates first. He needs to pay off his store card with the 19½% interest rate first, then the Vista Card at 15%, followed by the Discolor Card (13%), the truck loan (8¾%), then the student loan (6½%). Joe needs to pay the minimum payments on each, every month, while working to pay them down.

2. Joe has some savings. Look at the interest rates he's earning compared to what he's paying on his debt. If he's earning LESS interest on his savings than the interest rate he's paying on his debt, he is smarter to pay off the higher interest debt with the savings.

    *   But first, of course, he must pay Uncle Sam.

    *   Next, he should take the money in his savings and money market accounts and pay off the store card and Vista card.

    *   Then, he'll pay as much as he can to the Discolor Card.

    *   An exception may be for the money in the checking account. He may not want to use that, as it gives him a small cushion of available cash for emergencies, in case he needs it.

    *   The mutual fund money he might use, depending on the cost to withdraw it. (In Joe's case, the fees and tax consequences

don't make it worth selling that investment. We'll leave that where it is.)

- He can't withdraw his long-term money (401K and IRA), unless he wants to pay taxes and penalties.

- This leaves him with $1,950 left on the Discolor Card and the full remaining balances on the truck ($250) and school ($1,500) loans, $3,700 in total.

3. Joe then needs to give an extra effort to paying off his remaining debt sooner rather than later. He should pay as much as he can above the minimum payment on the debt with the highest interest rate until it is paid off. Then, he needs to take the payment he was paying toward the first loan and apply it plus as much extra as he can toward the second loan. When that's paid off, he applies the entire amount he was paying for debt to the next loan.

Savings Plan:

1. Once Joe finds life after debt, he can start to build up his bounty. He is 35 years old and wants to be worth $1,000,000 by the time he's 58. He'll be starting with his investments of a mutual fund worth $2,800 and $14,200 in his 401K and IRA combined, $17,000.

2. How much must he save to reach his goal? He could either ask someone with a financial calculator or go to the "Savings Calculators" section of fincalc.com, then "Becoming a millionaire." He puts in his age, how much he has to start with ($17,000), and when he wants to be a millionaire (age 58), and the average interest rate he might earn (he uses 8%). If his money grows tax free (in his 401K or IRA, tax bracket of 0%), he learns that he will have to save and invest $13,688 per year or about $1,141 per month (use 0% for inflation in the calculator) to become a millionaire at 58.

3. But can Joe afford to save $13,688 per year? Is it reasonable? To find out, we've got to get a handle on one more "starting place"—how much cash Joe brings in and how much goes out. Joe makes $55,000 per year and his after tax annual income is $35,750. After filling out his Personal Spending Plan (discussed below) he realizes that he spends $24,000 per year on his necessities and entertainment. That

leaves him with only $11,750 per year (not $13,688) to save. Another visit to fincalc.com, this time to "Savings Calculator", "What will my current savings grow to" to input his numbers. Joe finds that he'll only have $872,551 in 23 years. Poor Joe—not a millionaire. But by inputting different lengths of time he discovers that in two more years he'll have his million, at age 60! (And we haven't even considered the value of his condo by then!) Joe has other choices, too. By breaking down and understanding what he spends each month, he can make choices to adjust his spending. He can spend more or less in each category each month, depending on his objectives and how long he wants to wait to achieve his goals.

Enough About Joe—It's Your Turn

The first steps are to find your two starting places:

1. Your **Net Worth** = What you own minus what you owe

2. Your **Personal Spending Plan** = How much money you bring in minus how much goes out

Once you know these two, you can find out how much you can save each month to be able to buy your next car with cash, pay for your children's college or meet Joe in Bora Bora at the Convention of Millionaires. Want to find out?

YOUR NET WORTH

What You Own Less What You Owe

Take a look at the truncated (shortened) example of the Net Worth Statement below.

NET WORTH

What you OWN less what you OWE

Truncated version - for illustration only

ASSETS

ASSETS — What You Own	Average Annual Interest or Return Rate	Today's Date: Amount	Date: Amount	Date: Amount	Date: Amount
			Watch Your Net Worth Grow		
Cash on Hand - not in a bank or investments		$	$	$	$
Basic Savings: certificates of deposit, credit unions, money markets accounts, etc.					
Checking		$	$	$	$
Savings		$	$	$	$
...MORE ACCOUNTS ARE ON FULL FORM ON WEBSITE					
Retirement Savings: IRA, vested portion of 401Ks, etc.					
Account:		$	$	$	$
...MORE ACCOUNTS ARE ON FULL FORM ON WEBSITE					
Other Investments: stock, mutual funds, bonds, treasury bills, cash value of life insurance, etc.					
Account:		$	$	$	$
...MORE ACCOUNTS ARE ON FULL FORM ON WEBSITE					
Real Estate: market value					
Property:		$	$	$	$
...MORE PROPERTY ACCOUNTS ARE ON FULL FORM ON WEBSITE					
Vehicles: market value					
Vehicle:		$	$	$	$
...MORE VEHICLES ARE ON FULL FORM ON WEBSITE					
Money You Are Owed: tax refund, loans, family, friends, settlements, etc.					
From:		$	$	$	$
...MORE MONEY OWED TO YOU ON FULL FORM ON WEBSITE					
Other Valuables: market value					
Art		$	$	$	$
...MORE VALUABLES ARE ON FULL FORM ON WEBSITE					
Total Assets		$ -	$ -	$ -	$ -

DEBT — What You Owe	Interest Rate	Today's Date: Amount	Date: Amount	Date: Amount	Date: Amount
			Watch Your Net Worth Grow		
Real Estate: remaining mortgage balance					
Property:		$	$	$	$
...MORE PROPERTY ACCOUNTS ARE ON FULL FORM ON WEBSITE					
Vehicles Loan Balances: remaining loan balances					
Vehicle Loan:		$	$	$	$
...MORE VEHICLES ARE ON FULL FORM ON WEBSITE					
Credit Cards: remaining balances					
Major Card:		$	$	$	$
...MORE ACCOUNTS ARE ON FULL FORM ON WEBSITE					
Other Loan Balances: student, taxes, lines of credit, settlements, family, etc.					
Loan:		$	$	$	$
...MORE LOANS ARE ON FULL FORM ON WEBSITE					
Total Debt		$ -	$ -	$ -	$ -
Total Net Worth		$ -	$ -	$ -	$ -

You can download a full, clean Net Worth form at my website, MoneySmartHappyHeart.com. Some forms require a password to open. The password is "success."

Fill it in using your bank statements and other records. The extra "Amount" columns to the right are added so you can fill in your Net Worth Statement periodically and watch your savings and Net Worth grow.

> **Couples:** Work on this together, or one of you fill it out and the other review it.

Once you've filled out your cash, assets, credit and debt, plus the approximate average interest rates you're paying or receiving on each, take a step back and look at your big picture. Apply the same logic we used for Joe to reduce debt with your current savings. First, allow for an emergency fund in your checking or savings accounts. Allow three to six months of living expenses in case of urgent need. Then, pay down debt with additional savings if the interest rates you are paying are higher than what you will be earning (be aware of taxes and penalties to withdraw retirement savings). Prioritize the order of debt you'll pay off, highest interest rates first, second highest rates next, and so on. (If you don't yet have an emergency fund, split the amount you can afford to contribute, half to the emergency fund and half to paying off debt, until your cash is built up. Then, use the full amount to pay off debt.) Go to an online calculator (ex: fincalc.com "Credit Card Calculators") to find out how long it will take you to zero out your credit cards and debt. Use different monthly payment amounts to see the time it can take to pay them off and how much interest you'll be paying in each case.

> **Couples:** Come to an agreement on the steps above—the amount of your emergency fund, the priority of your debt to pay off, and the payment amounts.

Once your credit is wiped out, pop over to the "Savings Calculators" for how much you want to accumulate and when. Now, you know how much to stash away to own a million bucks, have the down payment for a house, remodel your kitchen, whatever. But is it reasonable for you to actually squirrel away that much every month? You need to know if you bring in enough nuts. Time to look at how much cash you bring in versus how much goes out.

YOUR PERSONAL SPENDING PLAN
How Much You Earn Minus How Much You Spend

Your Personal Spending Plan will help you understand very clearly how much you bring in and how much you spend. Below you will find a truncated version of a Personal Spending Plan form so you can get an idea of what it looks like and how it can help. The full form has more lines, clear directions and additional information to help you fill it out.

You can download the full form at MoneySmartHappyHeart.com. Some forms require a password to open. The password is "success."

This form looks like a budget. It is a type of budget. It is lengthy, but this is part of its charm. It is probably the **easiest** and most **accurate** format you'll ever use to understand where your money goes. Simply drop in your income and how much you pay for each of your expenses.

It's easy.

Because every type of expense you pay for is already listed out. All you do is drop in the numbers. You don't need to remember anything you pay for. It's already there. If you want to get a general picture of where your cash is going, enter your best guess for each expense. If you want to be precise, look through your records (your checkbook, credit card statements, online accounts, and filed bills) and fill in the correct amounts.

It's accurate.

Because virtually every type of expense you pay is considered, you get to see where it's all going and how everything you buy impacts your overall financial picture. This will bring to light your monetary black holes so you'll never again wonder, "Where could it all have gone?!"

Your Personal Spending Plan breaks down your costs by family member, so you can consider, and more easily remember, your own expenses, those of your spouse or partner, those of your children, and shared costs. It automatically calculates your outlays by category and even figures the percentage of your income you spend on housing and transportation so you can compare it to the national average (51%). The far right column is for your Smart Spending; after you fill out your spending "as is," you can go back and make adjustments to help you achieve your goals. Lastly, all the instructions and guidance you need to fill out this form are embedded right in the form.

On the next page you will find a truncated version of a Personal Spending Plan form.

Couples: Work on this together, or one of you fill it out and the other review it.

PERSONAL SPENDING PLAN
What you earn minus what you spend
Truncated version - for illustration only See full form at www.MoneySmartHappyHeart.com

	YOURSELF	YOUR PARTNER	FAMILY/ CHILDREN	TOTAL HOUSEHOLD	SMART SPENDING
			MONTHLY INCOME		
Salary – after taxes are removed – see paystubs	$	$	$	$ -	$ -
Social Security Income	$	$	$	$ -	$ -
...MORE MONTHLY INCOME CATEGORIES ARE INCLUDED ON FULL FORM					
Total Monthly After Tax Income	$ -	$ -	$ -	$ -	$ -
HOME & UTILITIES			MONTHLY EXPENSES		
Home: Mortgage or Rent					
Condo, HOA, Neighborhood Association Fee	$	$	$	$ -	$
Property Taxes	$	$	$	$ -	$
...MORE HOME & UTILITY EXPENSES ARE INCLUDED ON FULL FORM					
Home & Utility Subtotal	$ -	$ -	$ -	$ -	$ -
TRANSPORTATION & VEHICLES					
Loan / Lease Payment	$	$	$	$ -	$
Insurance	$	$	$	$ -	$
...MORE TRANSPORT & VEHICLE EXPENSES ARE INCLUDED ON FULL FORM					
Transportation Subtotal	$ -	$ -	$ -	$ -	$ -
FOOD & HOUSEHOLD					
Grocery Store Items – food, cleaning, health, etc.	$	$	$	$ -	$
Gas/Fuel/Fares - subway, train, bus, taxi, ferry, etc.	$	$	$	$ -	$
...MORE FOOD & HOUSEHOLD EXPENSES ARE INCLUDED ON FULL FORM				$ -	
Food & Household Subtotal	$ -	$ -	$ -	$ -	$ -
OFFICE					
Computer hardware – purchases, ink, repairs, etc.	$	$	$	$ -	$
Computer software - purchases, subscriptions, upgrades...	$	$	$	$ -	$
...MORE OFFICE EXPENSES ARE INCLUDED ON FULL FORM				$ -	
Home Office Subtotal	$ -	$ -	$ -	$ -	$ -
MEDICAL & PERSONAL					
Medica, Dental, Vision Premiums	$	$	$	$ -	$
Chiropractic	$	$	$	$ -	$
...MORE MEDICAL & PERSONAL EXPENSES ARE INCLUDED ON FULL FORM				$ -	$
Personal Subtotal	$ -	$ -	$ -	$ -	$ -
CHILDREN					
School Tuition	$	$	$	$ -	$
Baby Sitter	$	$	$	$ -	$
...MORE CHILDREN EXPENSES ARE INCLUDED ON FULL FORM				$ -	$
Children Subtotal	$ -	$ -	$ -	$ -	$ -
PETS					
Food / Litter	$	$	$	$ -	$
...MORE PET EXPENSES ARE INCLUDED ON FULL FORM					
Pets Subtotal	$ -	$ -	$ -	$ -	$ -
...MORE CATEGORIES OF EXPENSES ARE ON FULL FORM					
TOTAL MONTHLY EXPENSES (add all Expense Subtotals above)					
DISCRETIONARY SPENDING	After necessary expenses are paid, you can spend the rest at your "discretion" i.e., on whatever you want.				
ADDITIONAL PAY DOWN OF DEBT:	$	$	$	$ -	$
SAVINGS	$	$	$	$ -	$
PRESENTS	$	$	$	$ -	$
THE EXTRAS	$	$	$	$ -	$
...MANY MORE DISCRETIONARY CATEGORIES ARE INCLUDED IN FULL FORM				$ -	$
REMAINING	$ -	$ -	$ -	$ -	$ -
See full form at www.MoneySmartHappyHeart.com					

You will probably have no trouble filling in how much you spend on the necessities in life as you likely have records for them. You have the stubs from your paid bills, credit card statements, and your checkbook entries. However, you may find it a little more difficult to recall exactly how much you spend when you use cash (e.g., meals out, gas for your car, snacks here and there, supplies, magazines...). How can you accurately record what you spend your cash on?

When people want to lose weight and need to know how many calories they consume daily, what do the diet experts tell them to do? They're told to write down everything they eat every day for a month. Day by day and hour by hour it is impossible to remember every little thing we pop into our mouths. We live in the details. We can't see the forest for the trees. Yet, in 30 days, it becomes clear when we see it all written down before us. You can get this same clarity in understanding your spending habits if you write down every dollar you spend for one month. They count calories; you count cash. Just for one month.

COUNTING YOUR CASH CALORIES

There are plenty of apps out there that make it easy for you to track your cash. They are more or less complex, and may add additional services, like sending you a regular report on your expenditures, reminding you when your bills are due, protecting you against hidden fees, or just providing a basic cash spending tracker. You can do an Internet search to find plenty of choices. Here are just a few you can check out (that are available at the writing of this book):

Spendee - http://www.spendeeapp.com

Bdgt – http://www.bdgt.me

BigSpender - http://42apps.co/bigspender/

WellSpent - http://love.wellspentapp.com

Mvelopes - http://www.mvelopes.com

Level Money - https://levelmoney.com

Budget Ease - https://budgetease.com

One Receipt - https://www.onereceipt.com

Daily-Budget Calculator - https://www.freeswim.co/products

You Need a Budget - YNAB - http://www.youneedabudget.com

BillGuard - https://www.billguard.com

Mint - https://www.mint.com

Don't want to do the research or you like paper and pen? Use my Cash Counter form. (I've provided one at MoneySmartHappyHeart.com. Some forms require a password to open. The password is "success.")

Print this form double the size of a dollar bill, so when you cut it out and fold it in half, it is the size of a dollar. Make several copies, staple them together, fold them in half and keep them with your cash, credit card, or in your checkbook. Track your purchases by recording the date you make the outlay, the amount, put a check in the column for the category, then write a brief description of what you bought. At the end of 30 days, total up all the amounts you recorded for Transportation & Vehicles, Food & Household, etc. This short-term personal study will help you get your head out of your money trees and see your financial forest.

Note: If your files and checkbook aren't all they could be (that is, you laughed out loud when I suggested you look up your living expenses in your "files, credit card statements, and checkbook entries"), use a Cash Counter form to record all your purchases for a month, not just cash buys.

To give you a sense of what this tool looks like, a shortened version of the full Cash Counter you will find on the website is below.

Another way to track, or limit, your cash spending is to withdraw the amount of cash budgeted for specific categories at the beginning of the month and use only that amount for the entire month, no more. You can separate the cash into separate envelopes for different budgeted categories, if you want to be more precise with what you spend. Another method is to open a separate credit card for discretionary purchases only, then let the credit card companies keep track of your spending, and log onto your account throughout the month to see where you are with your spending. Of course, you'll want to pay this card off in full every month.

CASH COUNTER

Truncated version - for illustration only

Find full form at MoneySmartHappyHeart.com

Date	Amount $	Home & Utilities	Transportation	Food & Household	Home Office	Medical & Personal	More columns are on the form on the website	Description
							More rows are on the full form on the website.	

JUST A QUICKIE

Below you'll see a Quickie/Summary Personal Spending Plan form. This Quickie/Summary doesn't get into the details of the full Plan. Instead of listing out every one of your expenses, it has only the major categories. The two columns can be used like this:

Column 1:

Quickie— The Quickie Game: Quickly fill in your best guesses of your income and spending.

Column 2:

Summary—Drop in the accurate subtotal from your detailed Personal Spending Plan after you have filled it out.

Now, you have a short, accurate summary of your income and spending. Compare this with the Quickie column. How'd you do? Were your quickie guesses close to reality?

Find a clean Quickie/Summary form at MoneySmartHappyHeart.com. Some forms require a password to open. The password is "success."

www.MoneySmartHappyHeart.com

QUICKIE / SUMMARY PERSONAL SPENDING PLAN

See the notes in the Personal Spending Plan for an explanation of each line.

	QUICKIE	SUMMARY
	Fill in your best guess of income & expenses for you plus everyone else in your household **TOTAL HOUSEHOLD**	Drop in Subtotals from detailed **PERSONAL SPENDING PLAN** **TOTAL HOUSEHOLD**
Enter **Total Monthly After Tax Income**	$ -	$ -
Enter Monthly Expenses		
Home & Utilities	$ -	$ -
Transportation & Vehicles	$ -	$ -
Food & Household	$ -	$ -
Office	$ -	$ -
Medical & Personal	$ -	$ -
Children	$ -	$ -
Pets	$ -	$ -
Work Expenses	$ -	$ -
Debt Payments	$ -	$ -
Financial	$ -	$ -
Other Necessities	$ -	$ -
Total Monthly Expenses	$0	$0
Discretionary Income	$0	$0
Enter **Total Discretionary Monthly Spending** (Includes Savings, Presents and all the Extras)	$ -	$ -
Remaining	$0	$0

WHIP IT GOOD

You have arrived at a place where you know what you spend and where you spend it. Now check it out. Do you have enough savings in your Personal Spending Plan to achieve your goals? The amount you have on the "Savings" line in your Personal Spending Plan should be the same (or more) than the monthly amount in the right hand column, Total Monthly Savings, in your Personal Savings Plan from Chapter Two. If not, whip it into shape. Work it. Massage it. Where can you save? What can you snip? Look at every dollar you are spending and think. Make your changes in the SMART SPENDING column. Spend $300 per month on dinners out? How about $200 per month instead? Fill in $200 under SMART SPENDING. Do this with all your expenses. Then, rework the savings for each of your goals in your Personal Savings Plan, from Chapter Two, if you need to.

On the line for "Presents" in your Personal Spending Plan under the SMART SPENDING column, write in the amount that you can afford to spend on presents (as a monthly amount). Now, let's revisit your Present Plan from Chapter One. Go back to the "Amount You Can Afford to Spend on Each Present" column of the Present Plan and allocate this amount among each of the goodies you give throughout the year. (The total on the bottom of the right hand column of your Present Plan should be the equal to 12 times your monthly "Presents" line in your Personal Spending Plan, since your Spending Plan is done monthly and the Present Plan is for the year). When present days come around, you will no longer need to guess the answer to that age-old question, "Well, how much do you want to spend?" Now, you know.

THAT'S ALL THERE IS TO IT

I hope you see that getting a handle on your financial situation is not so complicated.

You just:

- Find out your starting place. (Fill in the Net Worth and Personal Spending Plan forms.)

- Determine your destination. (This is already on your Dream Card and your Personal Savings Plan)

That's it. Turns out the part people think is the most complex is actually the easiest. You've got a few forms. You enter some numbers. You add 'em up. Not hard. But there is a hard part. You know it. It's not the math. It is the actual physical act of keeping your moola in your pocket. "Busting your Buts" got your head in the right place. It gave you a foundation, the mental framework. Now, you need the down and dirty how-to's. You need the knowledge and the strength to keep your money yours. You need Chapter Four.

Chapter 4

TAKING IT DOWN

Let's get practical. You already know the one simple mathematical equation that rules the financial universe:

YOUR INCOME – YOUR SPENDING = YOUR SAVINGS

To increase your savings you've got to either increase your income, or decrease your spending. Since taking down your spending is easier than bringing up your income, that's what we're going to concentrate on, for now.

GETTING THE BIG STUFF RIGHT

The majority of your money goes to purchase a minority of items: housing and transportation. According to the US Bureau of Labor Statistics' latest Consumer Expenditure Survey, the average annual expenditure on housing and transportation is 51% of total household expenses. When you choose the place you're going to live, your decision affects not only the obvious mortgage or rent payment, but all of the related costs that go along with it. Investigate first the property tax, homeowner's or rental insurance, association fees, repairs, utility bills, and maybe housekeeping, pool and gardening services. The vehicle you choose not only saddles you with a monthly payment, but will also determine how much you shell out for auto insurance, annual registration, gasoline, repairs, and maintenance. Because your home and transport account for so much of your monthly nut, it is critical that you get these big things right. Do not overextend yourself on these items. Do not live above your means. Do not make decisions based on raises or bonuses you're expecting over the next year(s). No matter how sure you are of these increases, they do not always come through.

What is your Home, Utilities & Transportation Percentage of Income (calculated on your Personal Spending Plan)? Can you get it lower? If your percentage is approaching 50 or over, trade in your car for a more modest model or take public transport. If your mortgage or rent is weighing you down, do what it takes to break free. Get a roommate or move to a place that you can better afford (tiny house or apartment, anyone?). You will feel more confident every day knowing that you are taking care of yourself and your family and staying financially healthy. (If you are renting, the less rent you pay now, the sooner you will be able to buy your own home, if you are so inclined.) There are so many other necessary and fun things to spend your money on. Don't spend it all in one (or two) places.

While we're on the subject of cars, I'd like to pass along some advice on purchasing one:

First of all, squeeze every drop of life out of the one you've got now. Don't rush into buying new. At some point, you'll be confronted with the keep-paying-those-outrageous-repair-bills-every-month-or-buy-a-new-car decision. Here's the answer. Do some research into a new car (that you can afford). Find out how much the monthly payment will be. You can get this information by calling the car dealer, auto financing company, or your bank. If you are spending (or expect to spend) less than that monthly payment every month on the repairs of your existing car, then hold on to it. The problem is, you don't know what part of your car will conk out next and how much you'll have to spend to fix it. Take your car into the shop and have them give it a once over. This will cost you some money, but it is smart money spent. If your mechanic comes back with the somber news that your car's internal organs are about ready to give up the ghost, you'll know not to spend any further money on repairs and that it's time to invest in a new (or used) set of wheels.

What to do with your old vehicle? Most people consider two options—sell it or trade it in. Find out how much you'd get for it in either case. You have a third choice. You can donate it. You may receive a tax deduction for the full *Blue Book* value, whereas you would only get a fraction of that by selling it. The last car I got rid of I would have received $300 by trading it in, but by donating it, I got the full *Blue Book* value, $2,400, to deduct off my taxes. This saved me almost $700 of federal and state income tax I would have otherwise paid. See IRS Publication 4303, A Donor's Guide to Vehicle Donations for more information on donating your car.

Finally, when it comes to buying your new automobile—buy it with cash, if you can. If you've got enough money saved up, use it; you'll save thousands in interest. A new $27,000 vehicle, with 20% down ($5,000), financed over 6 years at 5% interest, will actually cost you $30,510, which includes $3,510 in interest charges.[15] The same deal, paid over 3 years (instead of 6 years) brings your interest down to about $1,700 (around half). However, if you can pay for it with cash, you pay $0 interest, and you've saved yourself thousands of dollars.[16] Unlike a house that generally appreciates in value, a car depreciates substantially as soon as you drive it off the lot, so when its useful life runs out, you end up with a hunk of metal, that's worth nothing, or very little.

One caveat on the buying/borrowing/saving/investing decision. At the date of writing this book, interest rates are at an all time low. If you think you can get a higher rate of return from investing your money compared to the rate you would have to pay on your loan, it may make sense for you to take the loan and keep the rest invested. But this only works if you will, in fact, invest your extra cash, and you will, in fact, get a higher rate of return on the cash you invested.

---

15 Calculation generated using "What would my auto payments be?" calculator under Automobile Calculators at www.fincalc.com

16 If you take the $3,510 that you so wisely kept out of the hands of the banker, put it away for safekeeping for 30 years or so (waiting for your retirement, earning an average of 7% annually) pre-tax you'd accumulate just about $28,500 to use to spend on the grandkids, cruise around the Caribbean, or to pay cash for the vehicle you'll need later. (Used Bankrate.com Simple Savings Calculator)

If you don't have this kind of excess cash lying around, make it the shortest loan you can afford. The longer the loan, the longer you'll be stuck in that debt-living, interest-paying trap. Instead, buy a car you can afford on a two or three-year loan. When those years are up and you own the car, continue paying those same monthly payments into your own savings or investment accounts. By the time you'll need your next car, you'll be able to buy it with cash. You'll finally be auto loan free. If you're not in need of a car just yet, start saving now for the new one you'll need in a few years.

If you can sock away $250 per month, (investing it with a 7% return) in six years, you would have about $22,000 for a new set of wheels.[17] And you would have saved thousands of dollars on the interest you would otherwise pay on the loan. If you can't afford $250 per month, save what you can. The moral here is to either buy your next vehicle with cash, or put down as much, and finance as little, as possible. The banks are doing well enough without your interest payments.

DON'T GO THERE

Humans have a few natural, inborn tendencies—eating, sleeping, procreating and I'm going to add, spending money. These are deep-rooted, innate urges that we all have and are nothing to be ashamed of. However, we do, at this point, have to acknowledge that if we want to alter our behavior in any of these areas, we are working against what nature intended. That is why curbing your spending habits is such an exceedingly hard thing to do. In order to achieve this very difficult task we will need all the help, tricks and techniques we can learn. The first of these will apply to many facets of our lives:

Don't put yourself in a dangerous situation.

You know you. You know what your weaknesses are. If temptation lies in wait at the mall—don't go. If it's the collectibles convention that calls your cash—stay away. Wherever there is someone selling something you want, make sure you are very far away. Don't tag along shopping with a friend, even if you are only keeping her company. Offer to meet her for lunch nearby, instead. Don't go window-shopping. Stay off the Internet shopping sites; say "No" to eBay

---

17 Calculation generated using Simple Savings Calculator at www.Bankrate.com

and the like. If you are trying to stop smoking, don't go to a party where you'd be standing in a smoke-filled room. If you are trying to lose weight, don't pass time in a donut shop. And if you're trying to save money, don't go to where the temptations are.

DON'T LEAVE HOME WITH THEM

Although keeping yourself out of harm's way is sound advice, it can't always be followed. You pass temptations on the way to work, on your lunch break and in the course of your daily routine. This is why you should keep no more money in your wallet than is absolutely necessary. Don't have extra cash on you "just in case." When you visit the bank, don't take out more money than you know will cover your needs. Try withdrawing a bit less than you normally do.

If you're deliberately going to put yourself in a dangerous situation just to "window shop," empty your wallet almost completely before you leave home. Keep 5 or 10 dollars on you. Don't take your checkbook and above all, leave home without your credit cards. Sign up for a gas card at a gas station. You'll be safe from running out of gas; you'll have a few dollars for a snack and another few dollars for an emergency.

Don't keep excess cash in your home. Your underwear drawer should not be more lucrative or convenient than your ATM. Just keep a very small stash hidden away for an emergency.

It really is true what they say about money burning a hole in your pocket. Few people know this fact, but the friction of several dollar bills rubbing against each other combined with the chemical makeup of the leather in your wallet, raises the temperature of the cash, making it unbearable for it to stay put! Your cash will look for every chance it gets to make a quick escape. The more money you have in there, the higher the temperature, the more desperate it is to flee. Do your cash a favor. Let it stay in the bank as long as possible, where it can stay safe, cool, and breathe easily.

LIVING LA VIDA BROKE-UH!

Are you living la vida broke-uh? Are you always living in anticipation of your next paycheck? If we took a snapshot of your financial picture right now, without regard to any income you'll be bringing in tomorrow or in the future, what does it look like? Do you have any savings? Do you have debt? I don't care that you'll be making more money next week, and I don't care how much stuff you own, if your debt outweighs your savings, you're broke.[18]

Do you feel broke? Most people don't, even though they've got credit card bills looming and no savings to speak of. So, why not *feel* broke? Because they have more room on their cards! How could they be broke when they can still buy?

Nobody wants to hear this. That's why people don't face up to the reality of what's going on in their lives and continue to fall deeper in debt and worsen their situation. However, let me be clear. "Broke" is not a description that describes you personally. It describes a temporary state that you may be in at the moment. You can deliberately change your condition. Stop increasing your debt, pay it down, then save it up.

> Don't make the buy
> If your bank account is dry.

THE SPIRIT OF PURCHASES YET TO COME

You want to buy something. What is it? Picture that item. Now picture it in the next room. The door's unlocked and you can go in and grab it whenever you'd like. There are a bunch of them in there. Actually, the room is piled floor to ceiling with hundreds, no, thousands of them. Maybe you'll go get one now. But since you can have as many as you want, whenever you want,

---

18 You may be exempt if you have equity in large valuable assets like a home, investment property, a boat, etc.

what's the rush? You can get it later or maybe tomorrow. If it's too available, we don't want it that badly.

If you want something and you can't have it—what happens? You want it more. You begin to think about it regularly. It stays on your mind. Your desire grows, and it can even become an obsession. The chase is on, and you cannot rest until you get it.

This phenomenon creates an unquenchable attraction to...you name it: homes, cars, clothes, shoes, toys, gadgets, food, desserts, and of course, the hottie at the gym. Ladies have all heard that old advice on how to win over the heart of your desired: "play hard to get," "let him pursue you," "don't be too available."

Simply thinking about something that's hard to get can make us happy. Psychologists call this "anticipatory joy." According to Emma M. Seppala, Ph.D., "Research by Stanford University's Brian Knutson shows that just looking at the object of our desire activates neural signals associated with the release of dopamine (a neurotransmitter released during reward signaling) in the brain. Dan Gilbert at Harvard has shown that we are terrible at predicting what will or will not make us happy and we often overestimate the amount of happiness something will bring us. Marketers play on our anticipatory joy by telling us that we will be happier if we buy or consume certain products. Sales, discounts, and special offers are nothing but a play on anticipatory joy."[19]

I'll never go on another diet again. I lose weight just by eating healthier. I can eat less, cut out carbs or even fast for a day, but the moment I decide that I'm going on a diet, and the second my mind gets wind that I'll be denying myself something—I become ravenously hungry and my mind cannot think about another thing except eating the next snack. Regardless that I just ate and I am certainly not hungry, if I am the least bit aware that I shouldn't eat anything more, I'll crave food like there's no tomorrow.

---

19 Quote from: How Desire Fools Us: The Benefits and Dangers of The Chase. Post published by Emma M Seppala, Ph.D., August, 2013 in Feeling it. Psychologytoday.com. https://www.psychologytoday.com/blog/feeling-it/201308/how-desire-fools-us-the-benefits-and-dangers-the-chase

So how do we quench these desires without giving in to them? Take the focus off. Picture yourself owning that item. Picture your life after you have made the purchase. Give this a try right now. Visualize yourself a few days after you have acquired whatever treasure you are currently lusting after. Now think about your life 3 months later. Has this purchase really improved the quality of your life? Is it actually worth all that angst? Where is your new gem? Does it sit on a shelf most of the time? Is it hanging in the back of your closet? In the bottom of a drawer? How often will you really use it? Once a month? Less than that? See? Once you can envision Life After Purchase, you can bring your desires back to reality. You will see that not buying is not that big of a sacrifice. Don't think of yourself as on a "financial diet," just live a healthier monetary lifestyle. Then, anticipate your real joys, your big dreams that deserve to be chased... and caught.

DO THE "WALK-AWAY"

"Pick up the phone and order today!"

"Call NOW!"

"Don't wait!"

"These deals won't last forever!"

"This weekend only!"

"Supplies are running out!"

Anyone who wants to sell you something also sells you a sense of urgency. They want your cash now, not later, not tomorrow, now. When's the last time a salesperson told you, "Look, take your time. Don't rush into anything. Go home and think about it. I don't want to see you in here for at least a week. Then, when you're good and ready, come on back in and we'll sell you whatever you want." Never! They know that many sales are made based on spur of the moment decisions and impulse buying. They know that if you leave their store there is little chance that you will ever return. And why don't you come back? Because you get home and come to your senses. You realize that there is more to the world than what that store holds for you. You start to lose interest and, very soon, you would have forgotten completely about that store, the nice salesman, and whatever it was he was selling. Walk away. You're in control, not the salesman. Gain perspective. If it was really an item you need, something you know you'll use and love, you can go back for it later.

So what do you do when you stumble into a store with all your favorites? Take a look around. Browse. Admire it all. Then, walk away. Now you know where the store is. You know that you can come back whenever you want. But for now—walk away.

Taking a picture may help. If you have experienced love at first sight, or your attachment has grown powerful during the last 15 minutes you've been fawning over your new object of affection, you may feel separation anxiety just ripping yourself away. Make it less dramatic and take a picture. Now, you can take home a memento. It's like a metaphorical piece of hair from your lover, kept safe and near your heart in a locket...your phone. You can look at it whenever you want. Chances are you won't look that often, then you can delete it and the other spur of the moment pictures you can't even remember why you took. This technique has saved me from countless useless foreign souvenirs that I would pay too much for, and would look ridiculously out of place in my home. I add these pic's into my photo album of the trip, and I can fondly remember them along with the rest of my travels.

What do you do when you've been trying on clothes all afternoon and have narrowed the choice down to your few favorites? Walk away. Come back for them later. If it makes you feel better, put them on hold. You need the extra time to go home and survey the situation. Does it work with the rest of your wardrobe? Is it a wise purchase to make this month? And, above all, keep in mind:

It will be there later!

It will always be there later. Perhaps that exact item will not be on the rack anymore, but there will always be beautiful clothes lining store shelves. There will always be more sports equipment, music, books, jewelry, movies, electronics, home decorations, kitchen aids, and personal luxuries to buy. They will be there. What's the rush? If you can hold firm and pass it up this time, you will gain that great feeling that you are stronger than your impulses and you can come back and buy your bauble at a later date.

The next time you go to a store or start the clicking to make an order...stop. Do the "Walk Away." Shopping online? Put it in your wish list or park it in your shopping cart. If you go back for it later, walk away again. Do it a few times with the same purchase. This is a great method to practice and strengthen self-control. If you go back for it a few times, at least now you know it's not an impulse: you really do want it, you will use it, and you've given it due consideration.

MANDATORY WAITING PERIOD

This is the advanced version of doing the "Walk Away." If you have a special something you want to buy, consciously put off the purchase for three, four, five, or six months. If you forget about it during this "mandatory waiting period," all the better. You really didn't need it or want it anyway. If you have truly decided to make this buy (and you know you can afford it), okay. Buy it. But give yourself four months first. Then do it. Write it on the calendar and look forward to it. Spontaneous spending can get you into a heap of financial trouble, especially when it becomes the norm. You can overcome your impulse buys. Make your purchases mindful, thoughtful acts.

> We buy things we don't need, with money we don't have,
> to impress people we don't like.

This quote has been credited to a variety of sources including Will Rogers, writer Clive Hamilton, the movie *Fight Club* and others.

THE LAND OF MISFIT BUYS

What do you own that isn't quite right: shoes that hurt your feet after a few hours, clothes that don't exactly fit or don't really go with your wardrobe, art you don't love, movies you rarely watch? How often do you ever wear them, enjoy it or watch it? Not very, right? It's just more stuff cluttering up your place. Aim to make everything you own, one of your favorite things. Don't own it if it isn't going to bring you pleasure and make your life more enjoyable for a long time.

Why did you buy it in the first place? Probably because, on some level, you're an optimist. You figured, "It doesn't seem exactly perfect right now, but after I break it in..." Or, "I'm not sure it will work exactly the way I need...but I'll give it a try...maybe it will."

Typically, we use our possessions most immediately after we buy them. Our excitement level is highest within the first few seconds of walking away from the register. Our glee fades proportionally with time over the next few weeks, months, and years. Our new treasure slowly travels from the shelf to the back of the closet, then into our "land of misfit buys." If your newest purchase isn't perfect when you buy it, the chance of it being an enjoyable and useful item over the long run are extremely diminished.

We tend to accumulate...stuff. We buy things because we're in the mood to shop, or it seemed like a good idea at the time. Our cabinets are bursting with things our years of toil and sweat, back-breaking and mind-bending work have provided for us. Look in that cabinet or room or garage filled with the stuff you never use. Picture piles of money in the place of this clutter, the money that you'd have instead of those useless items had you never bought them in the first place. Well, there's no need to cry over spilled money. You have a vast future in front of you and a fortune that will pass through your hands. Just make sure you don't make these mistakes again.

The first thing to do is clean it up. Have a garage sale or sell your stuff on eBay or Craig's List and put the proceeds into the bank. It may not be a large sum, but consider it personal reparations toward the amount you spent previously. If you figure a garage sale would be a waste of time, since most of your stuff is just plain junk and nobody would ever buy it—give it a try anyway. It is surprising what people will buy. I had a garage sale once where I had a few items I knew had value, but the rest of the trash I thought I couldn't give away. Within a few hours, I sold every single piece. True, toward the end of the sale I marked down prices to fire sale levels, but the point of the exercise was to get rid of it all. If it didn't go that morning, I'd have to pack it up in my car and drive it to the donation center. Better someone can use it than holding out for a few more dollars. And what a good feeling it is to have your shelves cleaned out and neat again.

Next, don't repeat the pattern. You work hard. You are pushed and pulled all day. You take direction from 15 different people who all want it done now, and you rarely get the credit you deserve. But you do get something. A couple of times a month, you get that piece of paper that reminds you why you do this everyday. That paycheck represents hours of your life. It deserves respect, as you do. Treat it well. Save that cash. Hold on to some of it and make it work for you. Make sure your years of labor pay off in the long run.

Speaking of accumulating, are you a collector? Do you know a collector? Obsessive collectors sometimes get their 15 minutes of fame on TV, showing off their enormous collection of dolls or Disney merchandise or cookie jars. I saw a program on a woman who collects bells. She has almost 2,000 of them. Is her collection done? Is a collection ever done? No. She'll keep buying her little ring-a-ding treasures and keep putting them up on her little shelves (that she needs to keep buying).

Beware the collection. If you've been thinking of starting one—don't. If you've got one already, enjoy it for what it is. Keep the additions to a minimum. Budget them. Only add onto it once or twice a year. Consider capping it. You can always buy more. But when does it end? What's more useful or important to you—another showpiece to add to your pile or to be the proud owner of a debt-free life?

During your next shopping excursion, faced with a temptation, think to yourself, "Do I really need it?" "Is this worth my time and energy?" "What will I do with it?" "Where will I even keep it?" "Is this purchase going to help me leave la vida broke-uh?" Samba right out of there. Keep it up and you'll find yourself living la vida loaded.

Shop with a critical eye. You are a discriminating and thoughtful person. You have high standards. Not just anything is good enough for you. You wouldn't buy just anything as a gift for a friend, would you? Treat yourself with as much care and concern as you do a friend. When you're making the "buy-or-put-back-decision" and you're not exactly sure if you'll love it—put it back. Don't buy it unless it's perfect. It's not good enough for you.

YOU WORK HARD FOR THE MONEY

Pop quiz!

You'd rather be:

- stuck in traffic racking your brain for some plausible excuse to tell your boss why you're late to work again

 or

- snuggly warm in your jammies with sweet dreams dancing in your head

You enjoy more:

- trying to function creatively and efficiently in your 11th hour of work with tomorrow's deadline looming over your head

  or

- relaxing with a good book and hot toddy in front of the fire

You prefer to be:

- sitting on a hard chair in your boss' cold office trying to make him understand the meaning of the phrase "a livable wage"

  or

- doing anything else, anywhere else, that doesn't have fluorescent lights, 10-minute breaks and an accounting department

The point of this quiz? To remind you of how very hard you work for the money. Every dollar you earn is well-deserved. When you spend these dollars you are making a judgment call that your time, energy, and expertise is worth that purchase.

Think about this. How much money do you make on an hourly basis and how much do you take home? It's different in each state, but 65% is a general approximation. How much does your next purchase cost? Now, how many customer-kissing, keyboard-punching, boss-pleasing hours of your time will it take to earn that amount? Is it really worth it?

But wait. It isn't that easy. First, you have all of your mandatory monthly expenses to cover. How many hours does it take to cover your rent or mortgage, car, insurance, groceries, etc.? You probably work somewhere between two and four weeks per month just to cover your basics. That means you have a few precious hours (dollars) left at the end of the month to buy the fun stuff. Choose wisely. Don't waste your time working off items that aren't really worth it.

Below is a chart that shows the hours it takes a person working full time (40 hours/week, 52 weeks/year) to earn the money to make a purchase. Find the closest annual income to yours down the left side. Move over to the right to see the hourly rate. The next column shows take-home pay per hour after payroll taxes (figuring taxes at 35%). On the far right you can see how long it will take you to work off a purchase.[20]

Annual Income	Hourly Income	Hourly Income after taxes	Hours (rounded) to work off a purchase of:				
			$50	$100	$250	$500	$1,000
$20,000	$9.62	$6.25	8	16	40	80	160
$30,000	$14.42	$9.38	5	11	27	53	107
$40,000	$19.23	$12.50	4	8	20	40	80
$50,000	$24.04	$15.63	3	6	16	32	64
$60,000	$28.85	$18.75	3	5	13	27	53
$70,000	$33.65	$21.88	2	5	11	23	46
$80,000	$38.46	$25.00	2	4	10	20	40
$90,000	$43.27	$28.13	2	4	9	18	36
$100,000	$48.08	$31.25	2	3	8	16	32

---

20 If you want to do this calculation for your specific income, divide your annual pay by the number of hours you work per year (for 40 hours/week, use 2,080 hours) to get your gross hourly pay rate. Subtract your payroll taxes (use 35%, unless you know your taxes) to get your take-home hourly pay. Divide the cost of a purchase by this amount to get the number of hours it will take to work it off.

If you're going to work as hard as you do, make it count. Use your working time to achieve the big stuff—the stuff your dreams are made of. Work hard. Stash some cash and get to realizing your goals—the real reason you're working—what you really deserve.

So before you write the check or slap down your credit card, think of how many hours it will take you to earn it back. Picture yourself at work, in your favorite monthly meeting, at your fluorescent-filled workstation, or dealing with your most difficult client.

Is it worth it?

You work hard for your money.

Make it work for you.

THROW AWAY SOCIETY

We live in an age of disposability. Everything is made for convenience and time conservation. You can throw it all away, from roast pans to contact lenses. It wasn't so long ago that when a rag was used to clean up a mess, it was washed and used again. Napkins, plates, handkerchiefs, and diapers were reused. Now, we make it all out of paper or plastic, use it once and throw it away. Hungry? Stop by the drive-through and when you're done you can throw away the plate, bowl, silverware, cup, straw, napkin and bag. The microwave has spawned a whole science of disposable food packaging. And almost everything you buy in the grocery store needs to be unwrapped, opened, then the container gets chucked out.

Because we live with so many of these conveniences, we are completely comfortable with the act of throwing away. Then, when one of our more permanent items develops a problem, our same pattern of behavior kicks in and we throw it away. Crack the habit. Consider the alternative: repair, don't replace. Reduce, reuse, recycle, and repurpose. Give our landfills, forests, and environment a break. Reduce your footprint and live more sustainably.

Search the Internet for how to make repairs; find yourself a handyman or drop it off at a repair center. Search images for "repurpose;" it's inspiring. The savings for a one-time fix-up or reuse may not amount to a lot, but over the years you will get to your financial goals sooner.

THE FAT CATS

Picture this. You're driving home from work. You've got the radio on, and you've heard a few commercials sprinkled in with the music. You've passed half a dozen billboards and as you turn down your street you notice an ad stapled on a telephone pole. You get out of your car and pick up two flyers that were dropped there by local companies. The mail is mostly junk: ads and coupons. You change into a "Nike" T-shirt. The dinner you picked up at the fast food spot has a "special offer" on the back and the soda you crack open allows you to get into an amusement park for a few dollars off. By the time you've read the paper and seen a little TV, you've been exposed to countless advertisements—and that was just since you left work.

The cbsnews.com article "Cutting Through Advertising Clutter" quotes Jay Walker-Smith, the president of the marketing firm Yankelovich, saying, "Well, it's a nonstop blitz of advertising messages. Everywhere we turn, we're saturated with advertising messages trying to get our attention." They add that Walker-Smith says we've gone from being exposed to about 500 ads a day back in the 1970s to as many as 5,000 a day, today.

We buy fashion magazines so the fashion industry can tell us how to dress and what to buy. Hollywood movies do product-placements, dropping name brand products in films so we will notice and spend. Luxury products are wrapped in gorgeous prints and floral designs because marketers have done studies and know what sells. Advertised restorative remedies have photos of calming bamboo and healing river stones on them, not because they will make you into a zen master, but because they are playing on your emotions. And, well, almost everything else is packaged with pictures of beautiful sexy women, because they are proven to grab your attention. Television commercials show the cutest little creatures. Awkward, puff-ball puppies and tiny, fluffy chicks tug at your heartstrings and grab at your wallet. Do you know who's behind those kittens and babies? It's a fat cat up in his penthouse office, lighting up an expensive stogie, and swilling down rare aged scotch— liquor that you bought him.

That fat cat doesn't care if you are putting yourself in debt to buy his product. He doesn't care that it will take years for you to pay it off. He doesn't care about you period. He's thirsty. He needs more scotch. And with this, he authorizes another round of TV ads, this time with even bustier models, happier couples, and, as if it's possible, even floppier kittens.

Be smart. Be yourself. Think intelligently and act independently. After all, this is what America is all about. Politicians claim to be mavericks. "Only in America" means only here can we do what we want and say what we think. Then, at the same time you're eating "freedom fries," you're pumped with the message that you're not cool if you don't wear certain clothes or carry the right accessories. You're not successful (read: desirable, in demand, lovable) if you don't drive the slick car or aren't seen at the right bar. Because we are dying to be desired, admired and loved...we fall for it. And the richie at the top of the corporate food chain eats it up. He has his driver park the Lambo in front of the chicest bistro in town, then steps out in his shiny crocodile shoes that, Oops! just got ruined because he stepped in a puddle! Oh well, not to worry. The driver is fired, and the personal assistant has just been ordered to buy him a new pair, which is couriered to the restaurant...because he's just got that much...of *your* money...that you keep giving him...instead of keeping it yourself...to make your own dreams come true.

You are a beautiful, intelligent, sexy, happy person on your own without those products. Don't give in to the pressure of the fashion industry, Hollywood, TV and magazines. Be a free thinker. Stand on your own. Western society is so solidly built on capitalism and the free market[21] that even those of us who do, very strongly, think of ourselves as unique and special have become status-conscious, fashion-slaving, restaurant-hoppers.

Don't compare yourself to the models and celebrities. They have agents, fashion consultants, and a PR team. Do you really need to conform to someone else's view to feel confident and accepted? You know what? You couldn't live up to their expectations even if you tried. They keep changing the rules to keep you buying more. But achieving your dreams is permanent and real. The next time you have the urge to buy what "they" say you need, picture the Fat Cat. He's lighting his cigar—with your money. He's blowing smoke—in your face. He thinks he's better than you. He's not. Don't bend to his will. Keep your cash. Don't let the commercialism get to you.

---

21 "Free market"? Have you ever seen anything in the market place that was free?

MY MOMMA TOLD ME:
"You'd Better Shop Around"

The number one responsibility of the chief financial officer of a corporation is to make sure the company operates profitably. Whether she's setting up a retirement plan, purchasing expensive high tech equipment, or investing excess cash, one step is always the same—she shops around. Her standard is to get at least three bids from different sources. This exercise gives her a few advantages—not only to find out who's charging what (and the price fluctuations can be surprising, for exactly the same thing), but she also learns the benefits of the different products, the level of service that comes along with each and the varying terms available. Then, after having gathered all this preliminary information, she goes back to the same companies and pits them against each other. Once they know that she knows their secrets (they've got a good product, but they charge 120% of what their competitors charge, for example) she's got them! She will also start to learn the downside of the products she is investigating. No one is going to tell her the problems with their own products, but you can bet the competition can't wait to spill it. Then, when she calls a company back, she brings up what she learned from the competition and makes them address it. She gets very valuable information this way.

Banks, lawyers, computer suppliers, insurance agents, almost all vendors, and stores will give you a better deal if you:

#1 - Ask for it

and

#2 - Tell them (if true) that you can get a better deal elsewhere.

Of course, there is a limit to how low they'll go. In fact, some companies may not budge a cent. But at this point, the CFO has all the information she needs and can make an intelligent and informed decision.

Apply the same process in making personal purchases. In some ways our lives are not so different from running a multinational corporation: maximizing income, minimizing expenses, spending what we currently need to have a happy life, yet planning and budgeting for the future. Before you spend your hard-earned money, you too should shop around. After all, you are your own chief financial officer.

If it's a major purchase (car, house, appliance, repair, renovation work, etc.) get at least three bids from different sources. Ask around. Call up friends. Use your network. Check out the reviews. A reference from a friend or coworker is sometimes the most valuable and accurate source. But don't follow it blindly. Get a few other quotes. Play them against each other. Tell them clearly and confidently if you can get a better deal elsewhere. Ask them if they can beat that deal. Then, after you've got a better value from Company B, call up Company A again and try the same thing with them. Now you're in business! You may get a better price than you would ever have dreamed. Plus, you may get extra peripheral goods, services, or better terms thrown in.

Who'd have guessed that momma was so right?

NEGOTIATION: A CRASH COURSE

ne go'ti ate" (ne -go'-she-ate): To bargain, offer, deal, discuss, debate, swap, hurdle, dicker, haggle, palter...

GETTING WHAT YOU WANT

Every day, all day long, we are trying to, above all, get what we want. Every person, in every country, of every age, and of every race is doing this. Every time we open our mouths we are saying something to get what we want. Even "Good morning" and "Excuse me" count; we are looking for friendship, happy relationships, a good reputation, etc. We negotiate in every facet of our lives and at all hours, not just at the office or on a sales call. In the department store when you ask if the towels are on sale, in the grocery store when you use a coupon, and in your son's eyes, when you are trying for the tenth time that night to put him to sleep, you are negotiating. Wouldn't it be great if you could do it better? If you could get what you want quicker, easier, and more often?

Did you hear, a few years ago, there was supposedly a book going around entitled, "How To Get Everything You've Always Wanted?" When you opened it up, there were 200 blank pages and only one that had written the words "ASK FOR IT." A bit simplistic, but the point is a good one.

The simple act of asking for what you want is the first (and most important) step in negotiating. As simple and easy as this may sound, it is often overlooked. Many companies and salespeople do their best to give the impression that they are inflexible. They have large corporate offices. They post their POLICIES, written in big black capital letters looming on the wall over you. They create an atmosphere of intimidation intending for you to never question their prices and quality to the point of feigning insult if you do. Don't buy it. None of it. Ask for what you want.

One hundred thousand people are raised one hundred thousand different ways. All of us know someone in our lives who is the most quiet, shy, timid, and retiring person we have ever met—someone who never speaks up and is easily overlooked. Likewise, we've all had a boisterous, obnoxious loudmouth in our lives. Someone who can't be ignored, as hard as you've tried, and acts like the world owes them everything. Guess who gets what they want more often.

We were all raised differently, with different values and different standards of conduct. How were you raised? To be assertive, and to go after what you want? If so, you're already ahead of the game. If you weren't, perhaps you've had a lot to overcome. Have you realized yet that asking is neither impolite nor brash? It is neither ballsy nor aggressive. And if you haven't learned this yet, it's time you do. I am not suggesting that you become an offensive idiot. Be confident, polite, friendly, and clear. Simply ask for what you'd like.

Once you've got this step down, you're well on you're way. We know now that you have a 100% better chance of getting what you want by asking, rather than not. A simple question may work—it's worth a shot. ("Excuse me, may I buy this waffle iron for half the price it's marked?") But there are ways of going about it that will increase your chances. There are a myriad of good books and videos out there that will teach you the ins and outs of negotiating and make you a haggling champion. Read up. But for now, here's a cheat sheet:

1. **Think about what you want ahead of time.** Don't just make it up on the spot. Create a range in your head: the price you *want* to pay and the highest price you *will* pay. Now, you clearly know your goal, what you'll accept and when you'll walk away.

WRONG	RIGHT
Thinking to yourself: "I sure would like that waffle iron. It's marked at $30. I'm going to see if I can get it for less."	Thinking to yourself: "I sure would like that waffle iron. I've seen it on sale earlier in the year for $18. I'll ask if they'll reduce the price to $15. The most I'll pay is $20, otherwise, I'll walk away."

2. **Don't quantify your request.** Allow your opponent to set the starting point. You may be surprised how much more you'll gain this way. I have received salaries, bonuses, and annual pay increases much higher than I would have asked for or expected because I didn't limit my request to the criteria in my head. This technique is most effective when you are really not sure of what the person on the other side of the table is thinking. If you want a raise, how high will they go? How much is the job really worth? Let them tell you. Understand that there are many factors on the other side of which you are not aware. Perhaps you feel you deserve a raise, and you think 3-5% is a reasonable increase. However, unbeknownst to you, your boss is willing to give you a 10% increase. If you ask first, you're guaranteed to get between a 0 and 5% raise. You've set the ceiling. Had your boss made the first move, she might have suggested 7%. Now, that's the floor. You can only go up from there.

However, there may be cases when you might want to start first. If you know what the other side will present and you want more, it may be better for you to speak first. If you are asking for a discount on an item in a store and you know that they will take 10% off, but you want 25% off, if you leave it up to them to give the first word, "10%" will be out there on the table. Then, when you come back with your 25% request, it will seem like a large increase from their starting point. Likewise, if it's time for an annual salary increase and you know that they'll give you a 4% raise, but you're gunning for 7%; you should name your price first. Once your amount is out there, a counteroffer of 4% will seem awfully low. They may feel awkward to even suggest such a low amount and counter with a 5 or 6% increase instead. You've already got them up from their original price, and you haven't even started negotiating.

If you want to negotiate the price of a product or service and don't know what to say, try:

- "Will you move on this price?"

- "What is your best price?"

- "Can you come down on this?"

3. **Don't base your request on arbitrary criteria.** You should have objective reasoning, based on fact and fairness, not just a sense of "I think I can get it for less." Do your homework and shop around. Find out what the market will bear. Although, I understand that there may be times when any discount will do. If, for example, a product has a flaw in it but is nonetheless acceptable to you, and you would still pay full price, then giving it the good old college try is fine and you'll get what you get.

4. **Talk to who counts.** Get the manager. Don't waste your time with anyone who can't make a decision. Don't even tell anyone else what you want. It usually decreases your chances of a positive result. The front person (the desk clerk or salesperson) will undoubtedly tell the manager what it is you want. The manager will have all that extra time to think up reasons why you're not going to get it. The manager now also has the added responsibility of showing his subordinate "how it's done" and the added pressure to prove his power and authority. Instead, quietly, politely, and with a smile on your face, ask for the manager (or the highest level person you can get). The smile will allay any fears of the salesperson. So when the manager asks, "What do they want?" her response can be "I don't know, but I don't think it's a big deal." When you get the decision maker, turn your back to everyone else and calmly ask him for what you want.

5. **Be confident.** Look him straight in the eye and ask your piece. Don't feel silly or squeamish. You have every right to ask, just as he has every right to say, "No."

6. **Smile.** Be friendly. If he likes you, you have a much better chance. Give a sincere compliment or make some brief small talk. Sympathize with him. Comment on how hard his job must be or acknowledge the pressure he's under. Be on his side starting out. It will be a refreshing change for him. People like the "Golden Rule" and typically do live by it, even if it's subconsciously. If you're nice to them, they'll be more inclined to be nice to you. However, don't be coy or forced. If you don't mean it, skip it. People would rather help you if they like you, but not if they feel you're being fake or patronizing.

7. **Never make it personal.** Discuss the issues only, never the people behind them. Don't make any comments about the person you're dealing with unless they're complimentary.

8. **Explain the WHY before the WHAT**. Explain your reasons WHY you are asking BEFORE you give away your position. You need to present your case before you summarize. By unfolding your side in this way, you are getting them on board slowly. They have the chance to agree with each little observation you make, before they even know that you want anything at all. Basically, you are giving them facts that they can agree with and leading them to the natural conclusion of your position or request. If you ask them for WHAT you want first, then explain WHY afterwards, you've lost your audience. Once you present WHAT it is you want (without having backed it up first) your listener will automatically be thinking up his reasons to oppose you and will not listen to the rest of your case. You are, then, defending yourself instead of guiding them along.

WRONG	RIGHT
"Excuse me, will you sell me that waffle iron for $15 instead of the $30 price it's marked? <<X>> Waffle World down the street is selling them for $17.50 and I see this is your last one, and it has no box..." <<X>> Right here the salesperson starts thinking, "Half price! Are you kidding? I've got a quota to meet and that leaves no room for my commission..." and doesn't hear another word of your good arguments.	"Excuse me, I was looking at this waffle iron...did you know that Waffle World down the street is selling the same thing for $17.50?" You've given the salesperson a fact. You haven't asked for anything. There's nothing for him to dispute. "I wanted this as a gift, but I'm told that this is your last one and you don't have a box for it. Is that right?" He checks and finds that this is another fact. He's thinking, objectively, that he'll never sell it at $30 and he's ready to offer you a lower price. If I pay you cash and take it "as is" can I give you $15 for it? You have a much better chance of success.

9. **Be quiet.** After you've presented your side, all of your reasons and then your request, be quiet. Silence is good. Many positive outcomes have been thwarted because the negotiator didn't feel comfortable with silence. Don't interrupt their thought. If it's quiet for a while, you've obviously given them something to think about. You may be winning at this point, but the next thing you say may turn the tide against you. Only use the arguments you need to. Likewise, if you've got the response you're looking for, but haven't expressed all of your reasons, keep the rest to yourself. You don't want to oversell your case. Pressing your point after you've won is humiliating and frustrating to your listener and may reverse their decision.

10. **Be creative.** Price isn't the only thing to work out. Also consider the terms (how long you have to pay, the interest rate, etc.), extra services, and additional options. Try to get a sense of what the other side's underlying motivation is and work from there. Money is not the motivating factor in every sale.

11. **Create a win-win outcome.** All parties involved should be happy with the results and feel good about the transaction. Negotiating isn't a battle, nor a droning debate; rather, it is an open, interested exchange, aiming to benefit both sides.

12. **If you've presented all of your arguments and you haven't got what you want, walk away.** Give them some time. They need some time to ponder your points, reflectively, by themselves. It also clearly illustrates that you are serious and are not bluffing. Let him sweat a little. You can always come back later. One technique that can work is to give the salesperson your business card and write the price you want to pay on the back. Ask him to give you a call when he's ready to match your request. Be ready for him to call you a few times with offers that start to approach yours. But hold fast. If he doesn't call you back with a final offer within a few days or weeks, you may be able to go back and buy it for his last quote.

A friend of mine used this strategy for buying a car and it worked beautifully. He also timed his purchase with the end of the year when he knew the dealer needed to make as many sales as possible to meet his annual quota. The salesman called him several times with lower and lower offers. My friend told him the same thing each time, "When you can sell it to me for the deal I'm looking for—give me a call. I hope to hear from you soon." Just before the end of the year he got the call he was waiting for and bought his new car for the price he wanted to pay!

The Art of the Game:

Just outside Nice in France there is a tiny village with cobblestone streets and narrow passageways. It is St. Paul de Vance, a magical and thriving artist colony.

My husband and I were on our honeymoon, and we had fallen in love with the paintings of an artist and wanted to buy a few, but the price of each painting was just too much to spend.

As luck would have it, we happened to visit on a rare day where the artist himself was minding the store instead of the gallery manager. The artist's major motivation was his art and its appreciation, not money.

We told him repeatedly how much we loved his work. He told us the meaning behind the images and where and how it should be displayed best. We left his gallery and returned later several times that afternoon, indicating that we're serious buyers, but also proving that we can and will walk away.

By the time the sun had set on that charming French town, we were the owners of two originals and two frames for little more than the price of just one. I was happy to get two gorgeous pieces at a terrific deal, and he was happy to have sold two of his most recent paintings, which validated the marketability of his new style.

A Note To The Haggle Shy

If you don't feel comfortable haggling or you feel it is too confrontational or self-centered, think of it this way—by asking for a lower price you may actually be doing the seller a favor. Just because a person owns a store or is the retail manager, doesn't mean he unequivocally knows the correct market value of every product. If you are looking at it, it obviously hasn't sold yet. Perhaps the price is too high, and he will never sell it for that much. If you want the item and are willing to pay a lower price, the seller may be happier to sell it to you for your offer than to end up with it unsold and make no profit at all. So by making your offer, you're giving him the opportunity to make the sale. If he's firm with his price, he'll say so.

Negotiating may not work all of the time, or in every situation, but it may work some of the time and in some situations. Why not give it a try?

CUT YOUR COSTS IN HALF

If you're not ready to go cold turkey on some of life's expensive little pleasures, cut them in half. Buy them only half as often. If you are in the habit of going out to lunch everyday, go every other day. If you dine out weekly, make it every other week. And if you treat yourself to a bouquet of flowers every other week, bring them home just once a month. The cost of smoothies, coffees, drinks, and cigarettes can really add up. Do a quick calculation. Multiply your average daily, weekly or monthly costs over the year. If it's daily, multiply the cost by 365. If it's weekly, multiply it by 52, or if it's monthly, times it by 12. Then, you'll get an idea of how much you're really spending over the year. If you can make these purchases only half as often, the savings can be substantial and you aren't really denying yourself.

Find out how much you are actually spending by using the interactive Cut Your Costs in Half form at my website, MoneySmartHappyHeart.com. Some forms require a password to open. The password is "success."

CUT YOUR COSTS IN HALF
How much are you actually spending?

Description of Purchase	Price of Each Purchase	Annual Cost
Daily:		Multiply price of each by 365
Total annual cost for daily purchases:		$
Weekly:		Multiply price of each by 52
Total annual cost for weekly purchases:		$
Monthly:		Multiply price of each by 12
Total annual cost for monthly purchases:		$
What you are spending per year:		$

Substitute

Cut your costs in half or just cut them down. Either way, over time, you can make a big dent. Enjoy your expensive pleasures in a much less expensive way. Substitute. Here are some suggestions to spark your imagination:

Expensive Pleasure	Substitute
country or tennis club	- meet-ups - place of worship - Sunday Assembly - volunteer - join a non-profit board - local recreation center/YMCA
premium foods gourmet markets	- farmer's markets - ethnic grocery stores - shop the sales
health foods juices	- make it yourself (find recipe or online video)
theater, performances	- have friends over for "movie night" - discount ticket service (online or in town) - call box office for day-of or other discounts - seats further back - smaller/local theaters
drinks, clubs, fancy restaurants	- have a dinner, dance, cocktail, wine & cheese, BBQ, pool...party - throw a joint party with a friend - go to the same club, bar, cafe, etc. & have just a soda, an appetizer, or dessert
hair treatments manicures/pedicures	- beauty school that takes on clients (students are usually supervised by a pro) - do it yourself - girlfriend time
expensive clothes/shoes	- designer discount or outlet stores - shop the sales - online deals

gym membership	- climb actual stairs - jog with friends or neighbors - free weights at home - workout app or video
massage or spa treatments	- meditate - home treatments - turn your bathroom, bedroom or living room into a retreat
What's your pleasure?	How can you substitute?

Enjoy the lower cost options precisely because they are getting you further ahead, because you are being more true to yourself, respecting yourself, and acting adult, instead of giving in to the stomping, grabby, little child who wants what he or she wants right now. Focus on the less costly things in life that make you happy...and the big, more permanent things will be yours.

In the face of temptation, I still suggest you consider, "How much is enough?" "Where will you even put it?" and to just "Do the Walk-Away." However, if the temptation is too great or you know that you're looking at something very special (if you don't have to use credit to get it) take the leap. Make the buy. Just make sure it works in your Personal Spending Plan, and if it bumps you a bit over, make up for it by reducing your purchases over the next few weeks.

When I am trying to lose weight, sometimes I can lose more by eating ice cream. Why? Because if I have a weak moment, I can crave ice cream like there's no tomorrow. Then, after I devour the delicious delight, I have a renewed sense of purpose (not to mention a few pangs of guilt) and I can stick to my diet in a more serious and strict way than before my creamy transgression. Consequently, I skip a few meals and eat raw vegetables with vigor, vowing to make up for my tumble off the wagon. I can slim down faster this way.

If you take a tumble off your financial wagon, it's okay. Just make up for it. Get back on track with stronger conviction. Feel the guilt. Guilt can be good. Sometimes. It's like the way pain works. Pain is not fun, but it serves a very important purpose. If you didn't feel pain, you wouldn't know that you had just put your hand on the hot stove. Feel pain—pull hand away. It protects us.

Like guilt. It makes us aware that we have done something we shouldn't have done. Have you ever thrown your cares (and wallet) to the wind and gone on a shopping splurge? After you got home, did you feel the guilt? Maybe you returned to the scene of the crime and returned some of your over-indulgences. Good. Guilt can be good. If you absolutely must crack, do it. Even enjoy it. But pull your belt a bit tighter for the next few weeks and make up for it. Get back on track and keep heading toward financial health and happiness.

DIY

Many retail stores markup their inventory 100% from their cost, but some products are marked up much, much more. As reported in the article, "Top 10 Retail Markups" by Dave Roos and John Kelly in howstuffworks.com (money.howstuffworks.com), you could buy 1,000 gallons of municipal tap water for what you pay for a single bottle of Evian. Jewelry can be marked up 50-400% and pre-cut vegetables may be marked up 276% over the cost of buying them whole. Clothes can go for 100-300% their wholesale price. And the premium on makeup and perfume is enormous. Roos and Kelly say that, "Makeup is mostly clay, with wax, oil, and fragrance added. Yet, these simple ingredients can run you $30 for a few grams in a department store. Make your own from natural ingredients."

I'm hoping this shot of markup reality may fuel a desire for you to do it yourself—and save a ton. You are clever, resourceful, and innovative, and even if you never thought of yourself as creative, with a little training and desire, you can make your own. There are more free learning opportunities than ever before. Take advantage of YouTube, videos, blogs, podcasts, wikihow.com, howcast.com, diy.org, instructables.com, diynetwork.com and many others. Just search the phrase "how to" then what you want to learn.

My husband and I have saved many thousands over the years by doing these simple DIYs:

- highlighting and cutting my own hair and cutting my husband's hair
- darning and tailoring our clothes
- having dinner parties and potlucks instead of going out
- hand washing instead of dry cleaning

- fixing our own computer issues
- doing our own planting in our yard
- serving drinks for friends at home instead of going to a bar
- cleaning and doing the maintenance and repairs on our home
- making jewelry

I have friends who:

- make their own perfume, skin rejuvenation lotion, makeup remover, cleaning products, greeting cards, or art
- sew their own dresses
- knit their own sweaters, scarves, and hats
- fix and tune up their own cars or bicycles
- bake their own fancy desserts, instead of buying them at a bakery
- bake their own cookies, muffins, scones, or breakfast/granola bars instead of buying them at the coffee house

What do you do yourself? What *can* you do? Join the DIY crowd.

Ladies, if you highlight your hair yourself every few months instead of getting it done at the salon; you could save hundreds per year and many thousands over the long run. Guys, as Napoleon Dynamite says, "Girls only want boyfriends who have great skills."

YOU GET WHAT YOU PAY FOR (OR DO YOU?)

Paying more for a quality product over the drop-dead bargain is often the better value. If it's made better, stronger, and with more attention to detail, it will last longer, look better, and you'll be happier with it for years to come. But be discriminating in your quest for quality. Many products are basically the same thing with the only exception, the price tag. Don't just assume the higher priced item is more valuable. This is a trick wine merchants have used for decades. They know that we instinctively associate higher prices with higher quality.

The Winning Wine

A good friend of mine was invited to a dinner and wine tasting party. Most of the guests at this affair had MBAs from prestigious ivy league schools are all doing very well in their respective industries, and all have a deep appreciation of good wine. Everyone was asked to bring a bottle of wine for the tasting. Each of them brushed off aged bottles from their wine cellars, uncorked valuable vintages, or stopped by their local wine dealer and picked up something special for good friends and the party.

All except my friend.

Knowing that her local Trader Joe's carries highly rated wines at very good prices, she picked up a silver medal winner that was on special for $3.99.

The wine tasting was done blind. No one knew who's offering they were trying. Each guest swirled, sniffed, and slurped, then voted on their fermented favorite. And which do you think, at the end of the evening, most people voted as the winning wine?

Yes! It was Joe! The TraderJoe's $3.99 bottle won the taste buds of a group of some of the most discriminating and educated wine-lovers! This humble, but tasty, $3.99 bottle beat out its more expensive competition.

Just because it's expensive, doesn't mean it's better.

The Best of the Best

I know a man who buys top of the line whenever he can. He purchased a home in Southern California that was in desperate need of new windows. Lucky for him, only weeks after he moved in he received a flyer on his doorstep advertising a local window vendor who only sells the highest quality products available.

My friend had the salesman come over to his home for a quote. Now, I feel that I can safely say that there will never be, in the continuing history of the world, better windows than these. They had indestructible, double-paned glass that could not be shattered with a sledgehammer. Argon gas was injected between the panes. Neither thieves nor noise nor the freezing cold of night could penetrate. Furthermore, the sun's harmful ultraviolet rays, which can cause fading of curtains, carpets, and furniture, are blocked out completely. The glass was surrounded by space-aged vinyl, and finally, the windows opened up and tilted in, so you can stay warm and dry indoors when you clean them.

My friend had his checkbook out and just finished writing the amount ("eight-thousand-three-hundred-dollars-and..") when his wife asked to see him in the kitchen. His more conservative-minded spouse gently reminded her better half that not only do they live in a very quiet neighborhood, and don't need premium noise controlling windows, but they live in Los Angeles in a one story house. Temperatures never get to freezing and it is always warm and dry outside, so no extra needs to be spent on superfluous features, like tilt-in panes. She also reminded him that this was their first quote, and they should probably shop around a bit before they commit.

After further research, the happy couple ended up buying good quality windows, appropriate for their circumstances, and spent $3,000 on the entire job. They avoided overbuying and saved a cool five grand.

Consider your needs and don't overbuy.

OFF-PRICE SHOPPING

I still believe that the benefits of smart discount shopping outweigh any potential problems. You can find bargains o' plenty at factory outlets, discount stores, sales at retail shops, online and even at garage sales and thrift shops.

Factory or Manufacturer's Outlet Stores

Factory outlets are great places to shop. If a retail store sells high quality products at high prices, the outlet of that same store may sell the same quality items at well-reduced rates. If you typically buy from these types of stores, the outlet can save you a bundle. If a regular store stocks products of questionable quality, the outlet may carry the same cheap merchandise at super cheap prices. And, if you can, like my sister, pick up a pretty skirt for $10.00, and get a few seasons of wear out of it until it falls apart, it is still worth it. One note of caution. Don't assume every item in the outlet is a deal. Although discounts up to 80% off retail aren't uncommon, the occasional higher-than-retail pieces or lower quality items made specifically for the outlet store are snuck in to keep the outlets' profit margins up. Consider each product and its particular bargain worthiness.

Discount Stores

There is probably an off-price store or catalog for every type of product you can think of. When I need to make a purchase, my first thought is "Where can I get the best deal?" My mind immediately goes to the warehouse, club or discount stores. To remind you of who's got what, keep a file with the pamphlets or notes (name, address, phone number and hours) of your favorite cheapies or just do an Internet search for "Discount Stores" in <your city>. Yelp has reviews of many of these shops.

Sales

If I'm not getting it at an outlet or discount store, I'm probably buying it on sale. I love to see the original price obliterated by the bright red half-off line. If there's no sale going on currently, ask the salesclerk when the next sale happens. If they know, they will usually be happy to tell you. Go to the clearance rack first when you go in the store. It's always in the back, so you have to walk past all the current full-price items. Put your blinders on and walk through. The biggest seasonal sales happen at the end of summer, after Christmas and early spring. (I waited until early summer and picked up a beautiful $400 black leather jacket for $99!)

Discount Apps

Are you taking advantage of the discounts available via your mobile device? In their 2014 online article, "9 free mobile apps that grab discounts and deals, use them in stores to save the most, our Shopping Strategist says" Consumer Reports introduces: Clutch, Favado, Goodzer, Paochit, Pounce, PriceGrabber, RedLaser, RetailMeNot, and Shopping by TheFind. Check them (and others) out to see which works best for you.

Online Shopping

Coupons: I've never been big on coupon shopping. I am not tempted to buy a product that I would not normally because it comes with a coupon for 50 cents. This is often their tactic; so don't buy more than you need because you can get it a little cheaper. That said, if you are a smart coupon shopper, check out the online coupon sites (you will generally need a printer).

Codes: Search for codes, which are like a printed coupon; you just input the code into your online shopping site (instead of printing out a coupon)

Rebate portals: are sites through which you access their retail partners. By funneling customers to their sites, they get an incentive and they share it with you, giving you a percentage back on your purchases (or points or miles) that you later cash out. A few examples are ebates.com, evrewards.com, cashbackholic.com.

Auction, Discount, and Resale Sites: There are the biggies: craigslist, eBay, Amazon and Overstock. Then there are smaller sites. Check out: swap.com, eBid.net, GovernmentAuctions.org, cqout.com, quiBids.com, happybidday.com, AliExpress.com, and DHGte.com. Search for the name of a store and the word "outlet," (including Amazon!) or search for the item you want and the word "discount."

Price comparisons: shopping bots compare prices and deliver sites and cost (ex: Shopzilla, MySimon, PriceGrabber, CNET Shopper for electronics, DVD Price Search for movies, Edmunds for cars, Priceviewer for top retailers). It's a good idea to use more than one and compare what they deliver.

The Federal Trade Commission has information about safe online shopping at http://www.consumer.ftc.gov/articles/0020-shopping-online. You may

also want to read about protecting your online privacy at http://
www.usa.gov/topics/family/privacy-protection/online.shtml.

Garage/Lawn Sales

Shopping garage sales are fun. You never know what treasure you'll stumble
upon. Because the motivation for private parties selling their excess is more
often to clean out than to clean up, the deals are unparalleled. Go forth early
and haggle. Ever watch "Antiques Roadshow?" I'll say no more.

Thrift or Resale Stores

Don't consider thrift and resale stores beneath you. They're not beneath the
woman I bumped into who was loading a beautiful antique table (she bought
for a song) into her Mercedes. My happiest and most recent thrift store
acquisitions are a Salvatore Ferragamo $800 blazer purchased for $100, my
now favorite cashmere sweater for $3 and a high-powered telescope for $12!

GIFT-GIVING

If your completed Present Plan from Chapter One made you realize that your
gift-giving largess should be a little less large, you may be looking for some
low-cost, high-value gift ideas. Here you go.

Write it up and Wrap it up: Anyone can make a rushed trip to the mall,
grab a gift and go. What do your friends really want? Deep down, what does
everyone want? Acceptance, friendship, love. Give 'em what they want. Give a
gift of your time. Take a day off of work, use a weekend, weeknight or
holiday. Take him to the beach, the lake, the hills or the flats. Take her on a
hike, to the museum or spring for a simple lunch. Spend the kind of quality
time together that shows you care.

Another way to make a gift of your time is to provide some desperately
needed help. Cut his grass, clean her closet or wash his car. What does he like
to do the least? What chore does she hate? Offer it once or once a month. If
your friend has a child, baby-sit one night a month and give freedom! The
best gift a busy person could receive is more time. And they say time is
money, right? They'll remember this generosity for many years after they've
forgotten who else gave them what and which shelf it ended up on.

Do you have a special talent? Can you play an instrument? Are you tech savvy, a great cook or a sports ace? If your friend has an interest in your specialty, give them lessons. Wrap up a small present that compliments your talent. If you're a cook, wrap up a whisk and a copy of the recipe you'll teach them. If you're a golfer, give a box of balls, some tees and lessons.

Write where, when and what you'll do. Make it a certificate or a scroll and put it in a box. Wrap it up and stick on a plump bow. Give a card and write your idea inside: make a poem out of it or just a few heartfelt words. This makes your time and talent tangible.

You're probably very busy yourself. We all are these days. That's what makes your gift so special. When they ask you, "How can you find the time?" Tell them, "I'll find time. You're worth it."

Make It Yourself and Make It Memorable: If you are lucky and talented enough that your abilities can produce an artful creation, use it. A one-of-a-kind, self-made present is much more valuable than the store-bought kind. If you can sew, make a tablecloth, napkins or set of towels. A handmade blanket or stuffed animal becomes not only a cherished baby gift, but also a keepsake that your friend will appreciate for years. If you're good in the kitchen, can some fresh veggies, mix up a flavored vinegar or oil, or bake a basket-full of cookies or breads. Any of these treats cost a pretty penny in specialty stores. Add the special touch that makes it a luxury, wrap it beautifully.

Take something simple and dress it up. Candies, soap, bath beads, candles, spices, loose tea, almost any simple item looks special and expensive when you wrap it in a swath of organza or a sack of satin. You can either go to an upscale gift store and pay five times the amount, or buy a few products in the grocery, drug or discount store and dress them with beautiful fabrics, paper or ribbons.

Creative Crafts: Is your whole family creative? Limit presents from everyone to the homemade variety. Put a dollar limit on this. Since the ingredients in a self-made gift can get very expensive, propose that everyone make presents and spends no more than a set limit.

Gag Gift: If you haven't got the time or the talent, if you can't make 'em loot, make 'em laugh. Humor is a great gift. People love to be the center of attention. A joke gift puts your friend smack in the middle of it. It conveys your special relationship. It shows that you are close enough to poke a little fun. Look in toy and bookstores. Gag gifts are not about the money you spend or the quality of the item. It's about the joke and putting your pal in the spotlight.

Public Displays of Connection: If you are headed to a birthday party, engagement party, bridal or baby shower, you have another challenge to overcome. Often, as the centerpiece of these events, the guest of honor opens up every offering and publicly lays blame for each. First they read the card:

"Nine months ago you thought maybe,

you'd have yourself a cute baby!

Love,

Susie"

As if that wasn't embarrassing enough, the connection is made:

"And Susie got me..."

(...as she unwraps the box...)

"...a silver-plated melon-baller!!"

Oh, THANK YOU Susie!"

And you are publicly displayed as either a high-class, good-taste, generous and close friend, or a stingy, uncaring cheapskate. Read on for a few ways to avoid the latter label without breaking the bank.

The Registry: The easiest way is to buy off of their registry. They will like what you get them, no matter the price. People usually include a wide price range of gifts in their registry, but you probably need to shop early, to get the pick of the presents. If you wait too long, the great lower-priced items may be gone. Pitch in with other friends to buy more expensive items on the list. (A quick note to those who don't like to buy from registries because you want to give an original gift: I'm afraid I have never talked to anyone who was registered but hoped they would get something original and unique.)

Listen Up: If your friend isn't registered how do you know what they want? You need to listen to your friend for about six months prior to their big day. I mean really listen. You may be able to pick up an idea for something they'd really like that won't cost much at all. People will clearly tell you what they want in the normal course of conversation. What has their life been like lately? Did they just buy a dog, a house or have a baby? Perhaps they've gone to a movie and really enjoyed the music. A sound track of that music would work. Have you been to their place for dinner recently? What did you notice? Be aware while you're with them. Have they been traveling? Could they use an accessory for their car? You've just got to focus and listen. Keep notes during the year of your friends and what you notice they'd like, then use the list for the holidays or birthdays.

Get Out There: Go to a specialty store that carries the type of products that interest your friend: travel, gardening, books, toys, antiques, clothes, computer software, home furnishings, tools, music, jewelry, liquor, sports, candy, etc. Once you start to look around low cost ideas will come. Books are great. Search for your pal's favorite subject. Check out audio books as well. Magazine subscriptions can be a wonderful gift. Not only are they well-priced, they will show up as a happy surprise 12 times throughout the year. And gift certificates always fit. How about a certificate for a favorite restaurants or a new bistro in town? Does he have a child? Offer to baby sit the night he'll use it.

The Intangibles: For those who either have it all or no room for any more, experiential gifts do the trick. Many attractions will sell gift certificates or open ended admission tickets, from concerts, live theater, ballet, museums and spa's, to movies, amusement parks, mini golf, go carts, horseback riding, skiing, skating and pool halls. Look for discounted tickets online.

A Brimming Basket: One way to make a few small gifts look more extravagant is to buy a collection of lower priced, related items and wrap them up together in a basket. Arrange the items on a cushion of excelsior or shredded colored paper. Wrap it in cellophane, add a bright bow and curly ribbon, and you've got a spectacular treat. A sports basket could have a headband, wristband, power drink, and a tube of tennis balls and maybe a gift certificate for an hour at the local tennis club. Make a beauty-basket with nice shampoo, conditioner, a pretty barrette, mud mask and nail polish. A stationary basket would contain writing paper and envelopes, a pen and some stamps. A cook might love some kitchen utensils, a garlic press, a potholder and a hand towel. Add some very inexpensive items to lay about with the gifts: candies, soaps, bath beads, packets of seeds, granola bars, depending on the theme. The extra cost is negligible and it's a fun way to fill up the space. Who wouldn't love to get a basket bursting with home baked goodies, packed with a variety of gourmet foods, exotic fruit, or full of sausage, cheese, crackers and a bottle of wine? A nice collection can even be put together from the grocery store. Compare the cost of your assembled basket with any that you would buy complete. The cost is a fraction, but the effect is the same.

By the way, don't buy an expensive basket. Find a low cost one at dollar stores, Target, Kmart, or a drug or thrift store. The best priced baskets are had at garage sales. Pick up a few and hold onto them until you need them. Other basket themes? Hot tea, coffee, or chocolate, cocktails, herbs and spices, nuts and dried fruits, dinner or breakfast-in-a-basket (the ingredients and recipe to your favorite meal), cookie or muffin makings, gardening (flower seeds and bulbs), work survival kit (mug, drawer snacks, aspirin, hand sanitizer and a tiny bottle of vodka!), movie night, sports, spa day, camping, fisherman, travel...would anyone appreciate tee-shirts, underwear and socks?

Season's Gleamings

Last holiday season, Virginia went to a friend's house-warming party. She brought a small basket overflowing with five shining, glittering ornaments. It was the hit of the party and didn't cost her $25.00. The host displayed it on her mantel and the other guests asked who brought such a beautiful gift!

Christmas and the Holidays (aka "It's Beginning to Look a lot Like Credit"): The holidays are a special time of year: stepping from the frosty outside air into the immediate rush of warmth, the sweet smell of pine and a crackling fireplace. Everything feels cozy. Your workplace is transformed with garland and a tree. Even the malls and shopping centers become magical, twinkling places. There is a childlike anticipation leading up to these special days. Everyone wants to do their part to make it more special: decorations for the house, new clothes for the parties and groceries for the gatherings. You've dropped a wad and you haven't bought one present yet.

Do you load up the credit cards in December and spend the next year paying them off? Do they ever get paid off? Or does the balance just keep rising? Use your credit card for $1,000 worth of candy canes and choo-choo trains, pay it down with a minimum payment of $25 every month, at an 18% interest rate, you will still be paying off that debt five Christmases later! Ho! Ho! Ouch! By the time you do pay it off you will have paid over $500 in interest. That seems more like a 50% interest rate than 18%. Break the holiday credit cycle. Let Santa be the one with a sack of toys on his back and get that financial monkey off of yours. Only "holiday" as much as you can afford:

Pollyanna: Be the one in your family to suggest relief for everyone. Each person picks only one name out of a hat and gets a present for that one person. You gather together like always. You eat, drink and laugh (or argue) like every year. The only difference is your debt.

Dollar-limit Christmas: Everyone buys presents for everyone, but no one can spend more than...the limit everyone decides on...on each person. If you have decided to become financially fit, tell your friends and family that you have a tight budget this year. You will surely gain their respect and may also prove to be the inspiration they need to do the same.

Not everyone needs to go along with the exchange. If some relatives are in a sound financial place, they may not want to participate. They can make the traditional expensive purchases for everyone if they insist, but try to get them involved. Don't discriminate because they are better off than you. Even Brother Millionaire should be accepted and welcome to follow the rules.

Double Down: There are times when you may need to spend some real money to get a particular gift. If you would normally give a present to your friend at the holidays and on their birthday, combine the two occasions with one larger gift. Make it clear in the card that the gift is for both occasions, then when the second one comes around, remind them of the gift you already got them in the card and maybe add a small item that goes with it.

Presents in Waiting: How would you like to be 60-70% finished with your holiday shopping by December 1 and spend less money doing it? How? Buy presents year-round. Designate a box "Presents in Waiting." In May, when you stumble onto a close-out sale don't just buy a terrific and great-priced item for yourself, also get one for a friend and stash it in the box. In July when you take a vacation, pick up some non-perishable local market treats you can't buy at home. And in October, go to the neighborhood craft fair and find unique, handmade goods. By the time December wafts around, your present box is bursting with novel, interesting and imported gifts. Plus you've got a load off your mind and the extra shopping time to boot!

Challenges to Present in Waiting:

Challenge #1: Tastes may change throughout the year.

Answer #1 - Tastes don't change that dramatically from one year to the next. You know your family and good friends. You know their style and what inspires them. They all have unique hobbies, homes and fashion. In the many years I have been buying Christmas presents in July, I have never had a problem because my friend's taste had changed.

Challenge #2: What if they buy themselves the same thing before it's gifted to them?

Answer #2 - True, your friend may choose to buy themselves the same thing at some point during the year. If you are clued into their purchase ahead of time, you may have to blow the surprise and ask them not to buy it. They'll get the idea that you already got it for them and get a kick out of knowing you got them a present. If they already made the purchase, you have some choices. Either ask them to take it right back, take yours back (if that is still an option) or if you can't, be a switch-gifter. Who else would like it? Give it to someone else on your list.

Challenge #3: Items bought on sale months before the occasion can't be returned if they're not right.

Answer #3 - If you're concerned that the gift you're buying may not be right months from now, either switch-gift or do some sneaky research.

Sneaky Research

Jason was in a bookstore just after Christmas. They had some beautiful hardback cookbooks on sale. Glossy, beautifully illustrated, $45 Chinese gourmet cookbooks were selling for $14! Not only was he excited to have found such a treasure, but he suspected that his sister would enjoy a copy of this book as well.

He told the cashier that one of the books was a present and asked if he could bring it back if she didn't like it. She said because it was on sale he only had 7 days to return it. Later that night Jason called his sister "just to say Hi." During the conversation he weaseled in the story about the marvelous book he found for himself (minus the part about the super low price).

Her reaction was so positive that he knew he had a winner. Had her reaction been bland or mundane he could have returned the book. Since her birthday was so far off there was no way she would have suspected that he was thinking about her birthday already and the surprise was in tact.

If, during the year you chance upon a wonderful something at a heck of a deal, pick it up and decide to whom you'll gift it later. Then when you remember a birthday at the last minute, you may have just the thing!

To make "Presents in Waiting" work:

- Have one area in your home or garage to collect them all.

- Label to whom each gift is intended before you put it away.

- Don't forget about your secret hiding stash of gifts!

Artful Giving: There are two presents in front of you. One looks sloppy. It's wrapped in faded paper. The edges are ripped and flailing. The other is covered in a gorgeous print, tied with a beautiful ribbon and has greenery and a real red tulip on top. Which one do you want? A wrapped box can be a work of art and people are naturally attracted to beauty. A gourmet chef once told me that much of a fine dining experience is in the presentation of the food. By creating an enticing package, you make more to your offering than the gift itself. You create an entire experience. The contents of the box, then, become a little less important. From the first impression, create a theme of beauty or fun or elegance. The smaller and less expensive the gift, the more significant the presentation. If creativity is not your thing, pay a few extra bucks at the store and have them do it. Either way, subconsciously, your friend will feel the time and energy put into that package. They will sense that they are important to you.

GET IN THE FAST LANE: INCREASE YOUR INCOME

If you are now inspired and want to merge into the fast lane on the road to financial happiness, step on the gas. You can accelerate the time it will take to reduce your credit, increase your savings and reach your dreams. Instead of working on only one part of the equation, kick it into high gear and increase your income while you decrease your costs.

At Your Current Job

Take on Extra Shifts: Offer to put in more time during busy periods when the company has a higher volume of work or during the seasonal or holiday crunch. Volunteer to take over work shifts when a coworker takes off sick or goes on vacation.

Work Overtime: If you get paid for overtime, ask your boss if he has any extra projects he'd like you to work some overtime on. Maybe you can assist your department getting caught up on backlogged work or help with a special project. Find out if there is any of his work you can "take off his plate." You'll get the extra pay and some major Brownie points, too.

Annual Raises: If you've been working for the same company and you haven't received a raise in over a year, it might be time to ask for one. Do your best negotiating. Remember, explain "the Why before the What." Lead your boss toward the natural conclusion of increasing your pay because of the great work you do. Put a list together of the money you've saved, and continue to save, the company. Translate the work you do into hard saved dollars. If you've cut costs by finding a cheaper vendor or brought in more sales than last year, it will be easy to refer to the bottom line. But if you're not responsible for the sort of activities that directly contribute to profitability, you'll need to be resourceful in making the money connection. Are you 20% faster or more efficient than before? That means they needed 20% less employees to do the same work. Their savings = 20% x your pay. Has a new system or innovation you created decreased downtime, improved client relations or increased morale? Did it translate into less staff, higher output or more revenues? Be specific and quantify—actually write down the dollar amounts and be ready to share this with your boss at review time. Be creative. If you have increased your responsibilities, handle more volume, perform more advanced work or have been given greater management duties, ask to be compensated at a new rate to reflect your advancement. Take a look at your current job description and compare what you really do to what it says. You may not get much traction if your only argument is that you haven't had a raise for over a year...and you still work there. Companies usually only want to pay for more—more productivity, more profits, less expenses (in this case, less is more).

Market rate is another consideration. Check with salary.com or other market compensation websites for average salaries for your job in your region. If yours is low, and you are performing well, you have an argument to make. Be careful, though. Don't make your request sound like an ultimatum. Make sure the company knows you are happy working for them and want to continue but have become aware that the market rate for your job is higher than what they pay you. If they value your contributions, they may consider your request. But, if you're not their favorite, I'd skip it.

During any career-related negotiation, never bring up personal reasons why you want a raise: you're buying a house, having a baby, your rent went up, etc. Your superiors only want to hear how you've become more valuable to them. And never ever threaten to quit your job unless you really mean it.

How About a Bonus?: Have you done a really stand-out job this year? Make sure it's known. How have you contributed to your department or company's success in a big way? Did you bring in extra business? Significantly reduce expenses? Saved your boss' bum? Did you cover another job along with your own after a coworker quit or was downsized? If you saved them a lot of money from an ex-employee's absence, it's only reasonable that you should receive a small share of the savings. Point out how much they saved, if you can. Again, quantify. Did you endure a particularly rough time that might deserve special commendation? Don't forget, asking is half the battle. I can't tell you what to say since you can only be successful when you use your own words and speak in a fashion in which you are most comfortable, but you may want to structure your request something to this effect:

- Intro: Be positive; you're happy to be working there.

- The WHY: Explain the good stuff you've done. The reasons why you should get a bonus. Quantify, in detail, how much money you've saved the company.

- The WHAT: Go for it! Make your request. Be polite and respectful; don't be pushy. Leave the amount open. They may come back with more than you would have asked for. Later, if they come back with less than you were hoping, tell them "...I was thinking that a fair bonus might be more like $X..." Then be quiet and let them think. You may get it; you may not.

- Whether you get it or not, thank them and look to the future. You're looking forward to working together, as a team, continuing to do what you can to make a great organization.

- Congratulate yourself! Most people will never be this proactive and self-assured. Employers love workers with a good attitude and who are self-confident (but not smug). Even if they only throw a few dollars your way, something is better than nothing.

Bonus Negotiation Example:

Dear Mr. Jones:

First of all, I want to mention how happy I am to be working here at Uncle Slappy's House of Hamsters. During each of the last three years I've taken on more responsibilities, have implemented numerous ways to increase our efficiency and profitability and have enjoyed my job a great deal.

As you are aware, this last year has been an extremely difficult one as our merger with Rats R Us has created a lot of extra work in my department. Not only did I cover all of my increased workload, I helped transition our existing staff with our newly added staff by running weekly meetings and organizing several team-building events, including the summer picnic.

As I believe I have gone above and beyond my regular duties in contributing to the company's success, I feel that it is reasonable for me to request a bonus. Please take your time to consider what you feel might be an appropriate amount.

I am looking forward to another great year at Uncle Slappy's helping this company remain a leader in the short-haired rodent rental industry.

Kind Regards,

Above and Beyond

Ready to Advance? Are you in a job or career that is keeping you down spiritually or financially? Do you have so much more to contribute? Have you thought about a new path, or can you accelerate the path you're on? Use indeed.com to bring job opportunities to your email. This is your time! Go for the gold!

Moonlighting: If you are not being worked to the bone at your current job, you may be able to find some time for additional short-term or part-time work. Around the holidays retail stores are in need of extra help. This is a fast way to boost your bottom line without a long-term commitment. Weekend, night and evening work may be available at restaurants, bars and local shops.

Part Time or Temp Work: Check the job posting sites, target company websites, and don't be afraid to make some "cold-calls" to companies where you'd like to work. Talk to either the head of the department you'd like to work in or Human Resources. Make inquiries as to what part-time positions they have available and follow up by sending your resume. You just may call right when they need to fill a spot and you will have saved them the cost of advertising and hours of screening and interviewing candidates.

Tutor or Teach: What can you do that other people wish they could do? You may have more marketable skills than you think. Even the everyday stuff like cooking, baking, gardening, basic home or auto repair, and sewing is valuable. I have many friends who don't know the first thing about cooking a pot roast or baking a peach cobbler, but they wish they did. Many of our contemporaries don't have a clue on how to fix a leaky faucet or give their car a simple tune-up. If you are lucky enough to possess some of these highly demanded abilities, you can provide much needed services by teaching some informal classes in your home or tutoring individual "students." All you need to do is set up a "course plan," that is, create an outline of what you will cover, class by class. Each class may be one or two hours long. You may choose to create a five-week course and teach your class, say, every Wednesday night from 7-8pm. If you don't want to meet in your own home, set up a friendly locale in a coffee shop or restaurant or at an available room in a school or office building. Talk to the owners of the place to make the arrangements. Also try contacting local extension and adult education schools, junior colleges, universities and learning centers to see if they can help you get started. Shops that sell related products to your class may be willing to provide a room for you to use for the added publicity and foot traffic you will bring in.

There are many other skills that people are willing to pay to learn. From musical instruments to computer technology to a foreign language to art lessons, from resume writing to self-defense to basic bookkeeping to tax tips, you can put your unique abilities to work for you. What is your expertise? Not only can you bring in extra income for yourself, you will be helping people learn new, necessary and enjoyable skills conveniently and inexpensively.

Sell Your Services: With today's rush-rush, convenience-centered, I-want-to-have-it-all society, everyone's time is consumed with running home after an extra long working day, picking up the kids, trying to fit in a little exercise and grabbing a microwaveable dinner. People are willing to pay for conveniences like never before. Have you got some extra time? Become a part-time entrepreneur: handyman, painter, seamstress, housekeeper, baby-sitter, pet-walker, pet-sitter, party organizer, auto repairman, tax preparer, gardener, car washer. Do you have an entertainment skill? Can you play music for a dinner gathering, entertain children at a birthday party, video tape or photograph weddings or special events? What's your expertise? How can it work for you?

Handmade Goods: "...this beautiful piece was made by a local artist." There's extra charm and cachet in that statement. People like to support their community and their neighbors. That "local artist" could be you. You don't need prior experience and no one needs to see your resume. Gift stores need unique, well-made products to line their shelves. If you can create crafts: art, pottery, jewelry, dishes, pillows, candles, dried fruits, jams, hand sewn napkins, runners, stuffed animals, dolls, crocheted or knitted baby things, blankets or woodcrafts—give it a try. Local stores often get their products from local folks.

You'll need to:

1. Be ready to suggest a reasonable retail price for your product. Stores may rely on you to set the market price. They will probably pay you about half of that price. Mark up is typically 100% from what they pay.

2. Call the stores and ask the name of their buyer. Ask if you need to make an appointment with that person or if you can just stop by when they're in the store to show your "line."

3. Bring organized and easily carried and displayed samples. If you have enough "in stock," you can sell what you have on hand, otherwise, take orders and deliver within a few days or a week.

4. If they're hesitant, you might suggest to the store that you start out on a consignment basis. They only need to pay you when they sell your pieces. This way they have no risk, and will be more inclined to try your yet unproven product. Once it gets selling, they may be willing to buy it outright and trust that it will sell.

5. Bring an invoice pad with you (you can get one at an office supply store). In case you get orders—be prepared. Write down the store name, address and phone number, the name of the store representative making the order and the quantity, description, price of your wares and your terms of payment. Have the person sign your "purchase order" and give them a copy.

6. When you deliver your goods, have the store rep sign for the quantity of product that he received. Call or stop by the store every other week to see if you're selling. Stay in contact with the store. Don't expect them to call you to pay you for what's been selling. They sometimes wait to hear from you.

Rent a Room: Have you got room to spare? Rent it out and add to your income by hundreds of dollars a month. If you're not sure how you'll like the arrangement, rent on a month-to-month basis. Interview potential roommates. Ask about their job, income, and lifestyle. You'll want to run a credit check, background check, call references, make sure you're taking care of insurance and legal requirements, take a deposit and lay down the law. You can use sites like rentometer.com, Craigslist.com, airbnb.com or zillow.com to get a sense of the going rate for rooms in your area. Be fully prepared and do your research. Sites like rentingoutrooms.com and http://www.wikihow.com/Rent-a-Room-in-Your-House can help and so can your local and state government websites.

Make sure you understand the laws that apply in your area. State websites are often your state's abbreviation.gov. For example, CA.gov. A local librarian may be able to help you find the site and/or the information you're looking for. Make sure you have a clear contract signed by both you and your new roomy.

A short-term rental may work for you as well. Carolyn, a friend of mine, and her husband, went on vacation to Florida and stayed in an airbnb.com room and paid $75 per night. While they were away, they rented their Southern California condo out on airbnb.com for $200 per night. They actually made money while they were on vacation!

Spring Cleaning: Sell your stuff online or have a garage sale. Clear out your attic, basement or garage and make a few quick bucks. Recondition an old piece of furniture and sell it. Get rid of unused clothes, toys...all that miscellaneous stuff that's cluttering up your place. Resist the urge to blow this extra bit of income; even if it's small, it's a start.

CHAPTER FOUR RECAP

In this chapter, in addition to ways to increase your income, numerous strategies on TAKING IT DOWN have been presented. Generally, they fall into these categories:

Rise above.

- Keep your goals in mind. Focus on your dreams over coveting short-term pleasures.
- Think strategically and independently.
- Be your own person. Be more genuinely who you are and accept where you are right now.
- Don't be conned or taken in by societal, commercial, or personal pressures.
- Avoid risky or tempting situations.

Enjoy the pleasure, but...

- substitute it with a less expensive option,
- DIY, or
- find it for less.

Did I miss any ways to keep your money yours?

Of course I did! There are so many ways to save; no one book or person could recount them all. You have the freedom and power to do what makes the most sense and feels most comfortable for you and your family. Use your own creativity and intellect. Tune into the myriad of ideas out there. You can save on certain expenses over a few years, then change it up and save in new ways over the next years.

This chapter has conquered the biggies, getting to the heart of the matter by tackling psychological reasoning, understanding, and providing tangible actions. When you *want* to save because you know you are thinking intelligently, acting independently, and living strategically, it's easy. When you are confident and love yourself more than you want to impress or comply, it's simple. When you realize the sad consequences of short-term spending and the incredible satisfaction and awesome feeling of freedom that comes from focusing on your goals, it's painless.

Implement the techniques you've read here and use them as inspiration to come up with more of your own. Pile up your savings while so many others pile on the debt. The tectonic plates in your mind are shifting, and the result is a mountain of money growing in your bank.

Chapter 5

KEEPING IT UP

How can anyone stick with the cause over the long run? How can we permanently change our habits when they are so ingrained? Our upbringing, education, and lifestyle have led us to where we are today. These factors, plus the people we interact with and the way we feel about ourselves contribute to who we are and how we behave. Everyday we basically repeat our same activities. Every time we perform the same act, we reinforce these same old habits, whether they are welcome or not. Don't we all want to change at least something about ourselves? But how is it possible to change when everything about our lives strengthens the patterns we've already developed?

It is possible! We all know people who have lost weight, quit smoking, controlled their drinking, increased their exercise, or saved money. Why are they so special? What have they got? They've got gumption. Tenacity. Stick-with-it-ness.

How can you gain this edge? A University of Washington study found that the keys to KEEPING IT UP over the long run are:

- the person's confidence that they can make the change
- making a commitment to change, and
- persistence

Only 40 percent of the respondents who reached their goals did so on their first attempt. The rest kept trying and trying. Seventeen percent were successful after 6 or more attempts.

Persistence

Three steps forward and two steps back still moves you forward.

It's all about time and persistence. What steps can you take to lead you toward your dreams?

1. Set your goal, make your commitment, and always keep it in mind.

2. Write it down.

3. Picture yourself successful and see yourself making it happen.

4. Access your built-in support system: friends, family and organizations.

5. Celebrate your successes and mitigate your setbacks.

Use the techniques below for KEEPING IT UP over the coming weeks, months, and years.

FINANCIAL REPROGRAMMING—INTROSPECTION

It's time again for a little introspection. Because of your interest in this book, I assume that you are either in debt, do not have a huge pile of cash in the bank, or you've got a stash, but it is smaller than you'd like. Why is that? Is this the first time you've considered the topic of building your funds or have you been trying for years and have just not been able to make it happen? What's been holding you back?

Although our opinions on any subject are the result of cumulative experiences; our first impressions are so powerful that they can override years of subsequent and even contrary education and our own common sense. Our initial encounter with almost all areas of life happened when we were children, and we observed how our parents dealt with them. Your early attitudes about love, sex, food, and money, to name a few, were originally formed as a tot. During your earliest years, did you start to form a mindset about money that led to unhealthy or careless spending, or was it a strong and positive experience that guided you down a responsible and successful financial path?

Consider the questions below. Write out your responses. By writing them down, you can gain new perspective. They are no longer fleeting thoughts that wander in and out of your head. You can change them, if you need to.

> **Couples:** *After* you have answered the questions in section I and II, A. below *individually*, share your answers and discuss. After that, read together the question in section II, B. and discuss.

You can find a Financial Reprogramming—Introspection form at the website, MoneySmartHappyHeart.com.

Answer the following questions:

I. For Everyone:

- What were your mother and father's attitudes about money?

- How did your parents deal with money between themselves?

- How did your parents deal with money with you and your siblings?

- Relate three early childhood memories about money.

- How do you think these types of early experiences influenced (and continue to influence) how you handle your money?

- If you have been taught, either directly or inadvertently, negative messages about money that have caused you to be less than financially savvy, what can you do now to undo this programming?

- How would you describe your current approach to your finances?

- What are your good habits with money?

- What are your bad habits or thought patterns about money?

- Finish this sentence: I've tried to save before, but...

- Now that you have identified what has been standing in your way, combat these obstacles head on. What will you *commit to do, stop doing or change* for your financial health? [Couples: Skip this last question and continue below.]

II. For Couples:

After you have answered the questions in section I above and II, A. below *individually*, share your answers and discuss. After that, read together the question in section II, B. below and discuss.

A.

- How would you describe your partner's approach to his/her/your finances?

- What do you think are his/her good habits or thought patterns about money?

- What do you think are his/her bad habits or thought patterns about money (if any)?

- How do you think they can be improved?

- What would you like to ask your partner to do, change, or compromise around your finances?

At this point discuss with your partner your answers to all the questions above—in both sections I & II.

B.

After considering your own introspection and hearing your partner's requests, what will *you commit to do, change, or compromise* for your partner's, and your own, financial health?

KEEP YOUR EYE ON THE PRIZE

What motivates Olympic athletes to train and sweat and push themselves every day for years on end? Certainly they get tired. Surely, they would like to take a break. But they don't. They've got their eye on the prize! They want it that badly! You've got to want it, too. Remind yourself again what it is that you want. What's on those cards pasted up on your mirror and rubbing around with your cash? That's the good stuff. That's your prize. Don't let it out of your sight.

How does a prisoner of war survive years and years of captivity? He never lets the sweet image of his beloved girl back in Missouri out of his mind. He keeps his eye on his prize. What is there to live for? Yes! Later life and happiness! Although I don't mean to draw a parallel between being a prisoner of war and saving money, we can learn certain skills from our GI. Why are you denying yourself, now? Why can't you buy whatever you want, now? Yes! The promise of later life and happiness! If that tough soldier knew there was no hope of a later life, he'd surely give up. If you knew that the grill of a bus with your name on it was heading your way, I'd say that would make this whole point moot. But both you and he plan to live to a ripe old age. Since you have a long and wonderful life ahead, you have to live your life today with that in mind. You can be much more comfortable in the future than you are today, if you make it happen. The little bit of saving you do now, every day, will bring huge rewards later.

This brings us to another, lesser used "But" that wasn't addressed in Chapter One:

"But what if I die before I retire, and I never get to enjoy my money?"

If you know checkout time is fast approaching, okay, spend up. But if there's a medical problem that runs in your family and your forerunners have died early, keep in mind that medical research is advancing daily. Diseases that were incurable in our parents' time are now easily treated. What advances will make our lives longer, healthier and happier in just the next 10 years? Don't plan for the worse. Give yourself goals to live for.

If your deathwatch has no basis in reality and you use the silly excuse of: "But what if I get hit by a bus, or I die before I can use my money?" To you I say, "What if you don't?"

SEE IT —BE IT

Recall your dreams again. What are you saving for? Close your eyes and see it. If it's a house, what style is it? Craftsman? Spanish? If it's a big trip, where are you going? Italy? Thailand? Will you be sending your child to college? See him standing up on the podium with a tassel hanging in front of his face. Become as familiar as possible with your dreams. See them as a future reality. How can you passionately pursue something if you don't know exactly what it is?

Now picture yourself walking in the front door of your new home, walking through the winding back streets of Portofino, or as proud as can be, squeezing the life out of your little college grad. How do you look? You are confident, happy, and, yes, a little older. Your head is held up high. You made this happen (without the crushing weight of debt or huge interest charges to dampen the scene. It's all yours—free and clear!). You can finally reap the rewards of years of intelligent saving.

Back here in the present, you need to see something else. You must start to see yourself now as that happy, knowledgeable, self-assured person. See yourself as thrifty, smart, and financially minded. Don't tell people you're hopeless when it comes to money. You're not. Not any more. Start to know yourself in a different light. Even if you don't believe those words describe you just yet, act as though they do. A teacher once told me, "Fake it till you feel it." Pretend to be who you want to be, until you are. Carry yourself like someone with financial savvy. If you need some inspiration, model yourself after someone you believe to be wealth-wise, someone you admire and is financially conservative. It might be a family member, a teacher, a banker, the president of your company or a business associate. If no one you know fits the bill, use someone you admire from history, someone wise, like Abraham Lincoln, Jesus, or Gandhi. If they were working to save money, what would they do? If you keep it up long enough, you will start to feel it, believe it, and become it.

Write down these phrases and say them daily:

I am a smart with my money.

I am in control of my spending.

My dreams are coming true!

Add or substitute other strong, positive, present-tense statements that resonate with you and affirm and describe who you want to be, who you really are and what you want.

Last thing: If you can also picture yourself making it happen, you're almost there. Picture yourself in front of your greatest money challenge. Now, picture yourself walking away. See yourself passing it up. If bad thoughts start to creep in, or if your suppressed mind takes over and has you running through the store laughing and tossing everything within arm's reach into your cart, shake it off. Start again. You are responsible. You're doing the "Walk-Away." Seeing yourself withstanding your temptations will lead you to actually withstanding your temptations. Take a second now. Close your eyes. See it.

SAVE WITH A BUDDY

One Good Buddy: Mutual support and understanding gets us through some of the toughest times in life. Have you ever commiserated with a friend about how hard it is to save? Where is she now? Tell her that you've realized that it's time you take hold of your finances and you're looking for one good buddy to do it with. It's always easier when you share the experience. Sometimes you'll need the help, and sometimes you'll be her pillar of strength.

Personal Coach: If you can't find anyone to save with you, assign yourself a personal coach, someone who will encourage your success and support you when you slip. You just need a friend with an available phone and an open ear.

The Enforcer: Empower your coach or buddy. Give her a job. How can she keep you on track? Here's one example: determine how much you can save either weekly or monthly. Then, she can be the collector of those funds. Give her a load of deposit slips to your savings account and have her collect from you a check regularly (perhaps on the 15th of every month). Make the check out to your own name as it appears on your account. Your buddy can send the check and deposit slip to the bank for you as she collects them.

Every-buddy: After you tell your buddy or coach, it may help to tell everybody. Ask them for their help and support. At times you may be weak; at times you may plain forget. If your friends, family, and coworkers know that you are dedicated to improving your financial picture, they can help you remember and stay on track.

PROVE IT TO THEM!

Wouldn't it be great to show everyone that you can be that person skipping off to France or buying a car with cash? No one notices the everyday stuff you buy. We've already discussed how you can continue to enjoy time out with your friends. No one is paying attention to what you're ordering. No one knows about your purchases or lack thereof. But you better believe everyone is going to take notice when you plunk down the down payment to a house or take some time off to visit Ireland! They think they know you—financially flaky, hopeless with your money. Show them what you're really made of!

FIND STRENGTH BY
WATCHING YOUR MONEY GROW

This is the way I got hooked. Every few months I would take a look to see how much more money I had. It was truly inspiring! Zero cash over 10 years will yield zero interest. But $100 invested per month earning 10 percent interest over 10 years will result in not $12,000, but $20,000! That's the power of compound interest.

Of course, there's no guarantee that you will receive 10 percent interest from your investments. Maybe you'll earn 3 percent or 5 percent, or maybe you'll earn 12 percent. And my example assumes you're putting away $100 per month. Maybe you can afford to put away much more than that, or, perhaps that's too rich for your blood. There are many possible combinations of:

1. The amount you can save per month

2. The interest rate you'll receive on your deposits / investments

3. The period of time until you'll need the money

Go play around with these variables using an online savings or compound interest calculator. They will show you how much money you will have if you were to save and invest a fixed amount per month at different interest rates.

FEEL THE POWER

You wake up one morning and decide to finally get serious about losing a few pounds and swear yourself onto a diet. This time it's for real! Then, later that afternoon, you scarf down three Double Fudge Ding Doodlers. How do you feel? Weak and powerless. But, if you were to look those Doodlers in the eye, walk away, and guzzle a quart of Glacier Fresh Spring Water, how would you feel? Strong and powerful. It is a feeling second only to stepping on the scale and finally finding that there is 10 pounds less of you to celebrate!

It works the same with all habits. If you decide to quit then fall off the wagon, you feel small and guilty. When you stick with it, you are in control. Why not live your life with power? The more small victories you win—negotiating a better deal, shopping around for a lower price, doing the Walk-Away, delaying your purchase for six months or telling the Fat Cat to go Fat Cat himself—the more control you gain. The more you practice these techniques; the easier they become.

The next time you use the tools in this book, you are not only

- benefiting from the immediate results of your actions,

- increasing your personal power and control, but you are also

- practicing to make the next time, and the next time, easier (and the next time...and the next time...)

So, if coming closer to your dreams doesn't keep you busting your own "Buts," think about how good you're going to feel in two minutes when your back is to the store window and you are walking away. And, if this feel-good reason isn't doing it for you either, force yourself to do it just for the practice.

KNOW THE URGE WILL PASS

As I explained before, the urge to spend is not a shameful thing. It is natural. Healthy, even. If we didn't spend, we would be naked, hungry, and living in the woods in Wyoming somewhere. The problem comes only when we can't control the urge.

What do we know about urges? They affect us all, there are a multitude of them, and they come and go. Wait! We've hit on something. Obviously, we do not experience all of our urges at all times. If it gets satisfied, it goes away. And the even better news—if we don't act on the urge at all, it may still go away. Even the basics like eating and sleeping may pass for a time. You might get super sleepy at the end of your workday. After you get home, have some dinner, and relax a bit, you may not feel tired anymore. You didn't sleep, but the urge went away. Our biological urges will eventually come back, since we would die without satisfying them. Spending, however, is not biological in nature. The urge may come, and it will go.

If you acknowledge the urge when it hits you, then understand that it will soon fade; you will have it under control. Keep yourself busy. Go on with your business. Do something, anything. Get on with the better part of your life that doesn't involve the participation of your wallet.

THE INCENTIVE PLAN

You've already decided on financial goals in Chapter Two, so you have something to work toward. Now, break up your ultimate goal into smaller, more manageable sections. If you have the goal to save $50,000, it may seem like a very difficult task. Who knows when you will ever accumulate that much wealth? But, if you break it down into smaller chunks, it won't seem so hard. Fifty thousand dollars is just 10 $5,000. Ten. That's not so bad. You can do that. It's no longer unachievable and timeless. As soon as you save

$5,000, you're 10% of the way there. Another $5,000 gets you 20%, then 30%, 40%...80%...you're going to make it!

Corporations give incentives to employees to coax them to reach their goals. If a salesperson has a quota to sell $10 million worth of product, she may receive incentives when she hits predetermined milestones along the way. When that salesperson sells $1 million, she is praised at the monthly meeting and is taken to lunch. Once her next milestone is met, she gets a certificate for dinner for two at a swanky restaurant. When she signs the last account that puts her over that $10 million mark, that big bonus is all hers.

Incentivize yourself. Create some milestones along the way and give yourself something fun to look forward to. These are treats that you don't normally allow yourself or have recently cut back on. In Chapter Three, you became aware of how much and how often you can ordinarily indulge in splurges and still live a financially healthy lifestyle (by planning for them in your Personal Spending Plan). Your incentives will be more or less costly, depending on your own financial situation and what you can normally afford. Don't forget to budget these incentives into your Personal Spending Plan. Create three categories of incentives, like those below.

> **Couples:** Get together on this.

You can find the form below at my website, MoneySmartHappyHeart.com.

INCENTIVIZE YOURSELF
Chapter Five

Category 1: A treat that is free or low cost

    Examples: **Your List:**

    Eat pie!

    Breakfast out

    Take ½ day off and relax

    Flowers for the house

    Go to a coffee shop and read

    Visit a nearby town

Category 2: More expensive

    Examples: **Your List:**

    Have lunch at a nice restaurant

    Concert tickets

    Sign up for lessons

    Tickets to a ball game

    The *good* scotch

    Gourmet cheese

Category 3: A real pleasure

    Examples: **Your List:**

    One-hour massage

    Five-course dinner out

    New outfit

    Sunset cruise

    Pair of Ray-Bans

    Day at the amusement park

Dole out these incentives to yourself when you have reached your predetermined milestones.

But first you need to predetermine some milestones.

Begin with your Category 1 treats above for your first stages of success and use higher inducements as you save larger amounts. (It doesn't make much sense to save $200 then blow it all to congratulate yourself.) Reward yourself more often in the beginning and space them out as you go. Once you get more practice, saving will get easier and you'll need fewer incentives. Seeing your money grow will be incentive enough.

Incentive When I Accumulate		Incentive When You Accumulate	
Category 1	$ 500	_____	$_____
Category 1	$1,000	_____	$_____
Category 1 & 2	$3,000	_____	$_____
Category 1 & 2	$5,000	_____	$_____
Category 1 & 3	$10,000	_____	$_____
Category 2	$15,000	_____	$_____
Category 2	$20,000	_____	$_____
Category 3	$25,000	_____	$_____
Category 2	$30,000	_____	$_____
Category 2	$35,000	_____	$_____
Category 3	$40,000	_____	$_____
Buy MY HOUSE!! $50,000		_____ !!	$_____

KEEP A JOURNAL

If you're not already in the habit of keeping a journal, every night before you go to sleep write at least a paragraph or two about your savings efforts. If you currently keep a journal, add a small daily entry about your financial successes, frustrations, achievements, and challenges.

A journal guarantees you a few minutes per day of quiet contemplation. No matter how hectic your life gets, you can always find five minutes just before you pull up the blanket and turn off the lights to concentrate on yourself. It also gives you a very effective outlet to express yourself. It allows you to get the noise out of your head and onto the paper. Write about how you feel: be honest and angry, or giddy and gleeful. You can then concentrate and analyze your issues and leave any bad or negative feelings on the page.

As you are making sure that you will focus on your finances and savings at least once a day, you'll be less likely to forget about the good savings habits you are building up. Make another copy of that Dream Card you made in Chapter Two and use it as the bookmark in your journal. If you had a bit of a backslide during the day, address it in your writing. How does it make you feel? What are you going to do about it? Cinch your wallet in tighter for the next few weeks? Return your purchases? Reread "Busting the Buts" or "Taking it Down?" If you had success that day, celebrate! Write it down! Lavish complements and back-patting all over your smart self.

SELF-DISCIPLINE: The Ability to Make Yourself Do Things That Should Be Done

This definition comes from Merriam-Webster.com.

Before we part I've added a section on good, old-fashioned self-control. If it were easy, we'd all be skinny, rich, well-read, muscle-bound, T-totalers with sparkling clean houses and that novel (or screenplay) in the hands of an agent. And almost all self-help books would never have been published because people would not need them to do what we know should be done.

The American Psychological Association's article, "What You Need to Know about Willpower: The Psychological Science to Self-Control,[22]" describes research conducted on self-discipline. In one study by University of Pennsylvania psychologists Angela Duckworth, PhD, and Martin Seligman, PhD, results found that the eighth-grade students who delayed receiving money ($2 if they waited a week versus $1 offered up front) got better grades, better school attendance, better standardized test scores and generally beat out other children in admittance to a competitive high school. They even found that self-discipline was a better predictor of academic success than IQ.

In another study by June Tangney, PhD, and her colleagues from George Mason University, a correlation was found between higher self-control in undergraduate students and better grade-point averages, more self-esteem, higher relationship skills, and less binge eating and alcohol abuse. And Terrie Moffitt, PhD, and colleagues, of Duke University, who tracked 1,000 people in Dunedin, New Zealand, from birth to age 32, found that those with high self-control as children became adults with, "...greater physical and mental health, fewer substance-abuse problems and criminal convictions, and better savings behavior and financial security."

Self-control is like a muscle, say researchers. Keep using it and it gets stronger. This has been proven in multiple studies. According to Roy Baumeister, PhD, psychologist and willpower researcher at Florida State University, once good habits are established, they become routine, and we don't need to think about them or exert the effort we had to when we were building them up.

In Forbes.com, "5 Proven Methods For Gaining Self Discipline"[23] by Jennifer Cohen, Wilhelm Hoffman's 2013 study indicates that more self-control makes people happier because these individuals are better able to overcome challenges they face while working to achieve their goals. They don't get derailed because of feelings or impulses, so it is easier to make more informed and better decisions and experience less stress.

---

22 http://www.apa.org/helpcenter/willpower.aspx

23 http://www.forbes.com/sites/jennifercohen/2014/06/18/5-proven-methods-for-gaining-self-discipline/

The American Psychological Association's article mentioned above suggests you can strengthen willpower by avoiding temptation and putting a plan in place before your will is tested. It also advocates setting clear goals, monitoring yourself regularly and practicing. Forbes.com also reports that self-discipline can be learned and requires practice. It suggests these five techniques to enhance resolve:

1. remove temptations,

2. eat healthfully and regularly, so your brain and mood are optimized and you can make smarter decisions,

3. push through the odd feeling that your routine has changed. It has and that's good. It will feel natural after you have created a habit, and your brain recognizes it as the new normal.

4. ease into it by scheduling breaks and rewarding yourself, and

5. forgive yourself and move forward when you hit a setback. Get back to it and continue your determination until a habit is formed.

This book provides a wealth of strategies, devices, and tools on how to put much of this research into practice.

KEEP THIS BOOK BY YOUR BED...

...and refer to it often. Dog ear the pages, highlight paragraphs, write notes all over the margins or printout key sections. In it find inspiration when you are weak and remind yourself when you forget. This book is designed as a reference and a guide to help you achieve your dreams. Keep it somewhere you will notice it daily and move it to a new place when you no longer see it because it has become part of the background.

Read more books on how to handle your money.

There are lots of books that will give you invaluable advice. Keep expanding your knowledge base on this topic. I have given you the basis to accumulate wealth. But once it starts to grow, you will want to know more about decreasing your taxes, what investments are right for you, writing a will, insurance, estate planning (for the enormous estate you will be leaving behind), etc. Shoot for reading one or two books on personal finances per year. After the health of yourself and your family, this is one of the most important matters in your life.

PROOF YOU CAN DO IT

I don't know you. I don't know anything about you. So how can I be so bold as to presume that I can actually prove that you can do this? Although I don't know what kind of person you are, I do know that if you are the kind of person who has ever held down a job, kept in shape, earned a degree, had a successful relationship, competed in sports, played an instrument or planted a garden, you can be successful with your money. How? Because the skills you need for financial success are exactly the same skills you already possess that have allowed you to excel in these other areas.

Work: It's true, I don't know you, but I do know that you have massive amounts of self-control. Have you ever cussed out your boss? Has he or she ever deserved it? Then why didn't you? It would be a lot of fun, right? You don't because there would be an immediate negative repercussion. You focus on the long-term benefits of not cussing out your boss. Your continuing paychecks convince you to keep quiet. Same with money. You could spend it recklessly, without regard to the long-term negative consequences. But that would not be smart. You need to consider the repercussions of your actions. Unlike telling off your manager, the unpleasant effects of spending your money may not be so immediate. This is why it is easier to spend your way into debt then to cuss your way into unemployment. However, you must acknowledge that the consequences are just as real and will catch up with you soon.

Exercise: It's surely not fun while you do it, especially in the beginning. You do it for the benefits for your mind and body. As you continue, it gets easier and easier. Then, it becomes a habit. You feel good afterwards because you know you're taking care of yourself. You also have a goal. You're working toward something—losing 10 pounds or keeping fit. Same with savings. You've got a goal. Keep it up and it gets easier.

Relationships: You want a good relationship. You want your partner to treat you with respect, kindness, and warmth. You want them to be there for you when you need them. What's your part in this equation? Can you do whatever you want to according to your every whim? No. You have obligations as well. You need to treat them well, respect them, and be there for them, too. You have a special place for them in your heart. Same with your money. If you want it to be there for you when you really need it, you must do your part. Respect it and have a special place for it—in your bank.

Playing A Musical Instrument: To become an accomplished musician you need to practice. Maybe for that hour or so every day you would rather be doing something else. Your friends might be calling you to join them. But you can't, you have to practice. After a few years, though, your dedication pays off. You can play Beethoven's beautiful concertos or improvise the blues with the band. Then, it becomes your friends who are impressed...and jealous. Just like money. Do what it takes; save a little bit each day. Sure, it would be more fun to be out shopping with your friends, but after a few years you get the payoff (and they'll be jealous).

Sports: You're in hot competition. You want to beat the other team. You want to crush your opponent. How do you do it? What does the coach tell you to do? Practice. Practice. Practice. You have got to get on the field regularly and do those rep's. No, it's not that much fun. Yes, it is a necessary step to achieving your goal. You know it and you're willing to do it. Same with saving. Just Do It.

A Garden: When you start your garden in the early spring, you do some initial work. All through the season you lovingly tend and maintain it. If you do the work that it takes to keep it healthy and thriving, it will pay off in spades. First, you get to enjoy the flowers, then the fruit. That fruit tastes so much better than the store bought stuff because you know you created it. Your love and work is in there. You would never pick the fruit before it's ripe, would you? You may be tempted. It may look big enough, just about ripe. You know what happens when you bite in too early. It's sour. Just like saving. You need to do some initial work by setting up your accounts and choosing some investments, then you need to tend it by stashing it away. Even though you may be tempted to spend the fruit of your savings before it's ready, don't do it. It will be much tastier when it is ripe, and you can start your business or see what kind of gardens they grow in England.

The Proof Inside of You

Your proof is inside of you. Take a minute, find them, and write them down.

Think about your successes. What have you accomplished in your life?

You did that.

You can do this, too.

7 SIMPLE STEPS - The *Money Smart, Happy Heart* Model For Financial Success

Putting it all Together

The lessons in this book have been condensed into the straightforward visual model below that plainly presents what it takes to build wealth, have the big things money can buy and feel fulfilled, happy and confident along the way. The steps do not directly correspond to each chapter, rather, they extract the major messages that run throughout the book. The information in this book is ordered to get right into the stories we tell ourselves about money, how to overcome certain blocks and get your head in the right place. Then, you did some dreaming by setting financial and life goals and you learned what the research says about how to feel happy and fulfilled. From there, you got a handle on your current financial picture, got strategies on how to take it down, then keep it up over the long run. The following model summarizes essential concepts and fundamental themes that are expressed throughout.

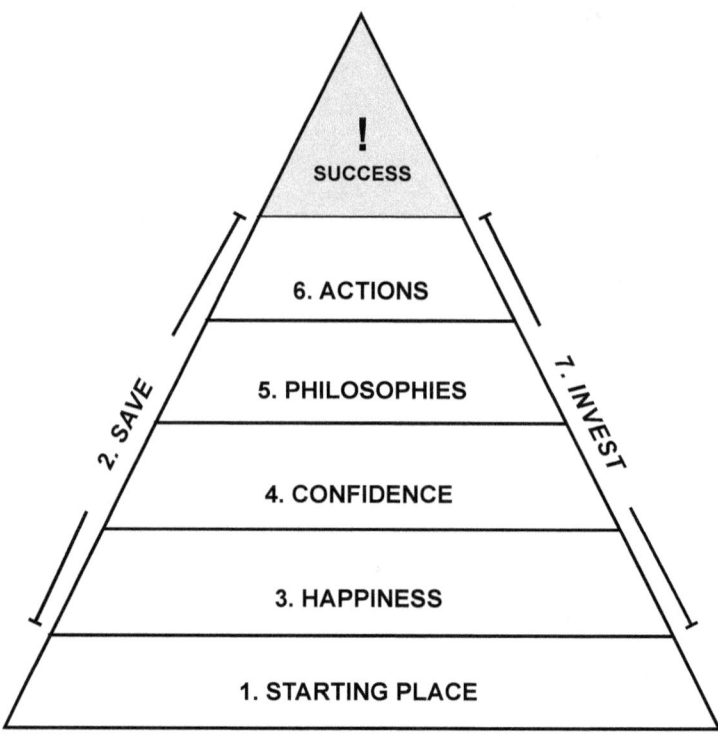

The seven simple steps on this pyramid work together, and each is an essential part of the program. Saving and investing flank most of the layers. They are of overriding importance and the tiers between them instruct *how* to get to the end of each month with money to save and invest. Your starting place is the block they all rest upon, although this step does not necessarily need to be done before the others. Start saving and investing as much as possible as soon as you can; this is key. Success is at the pinnacle! It is not one of the steps, per se, rather it is what you are working toward, your result...your awesome payoff! Use this model to help you put it all together, organize your thoughts, inform your action plan, and check that you're on track and employing each element. Let's unpack these steps and put it all together:

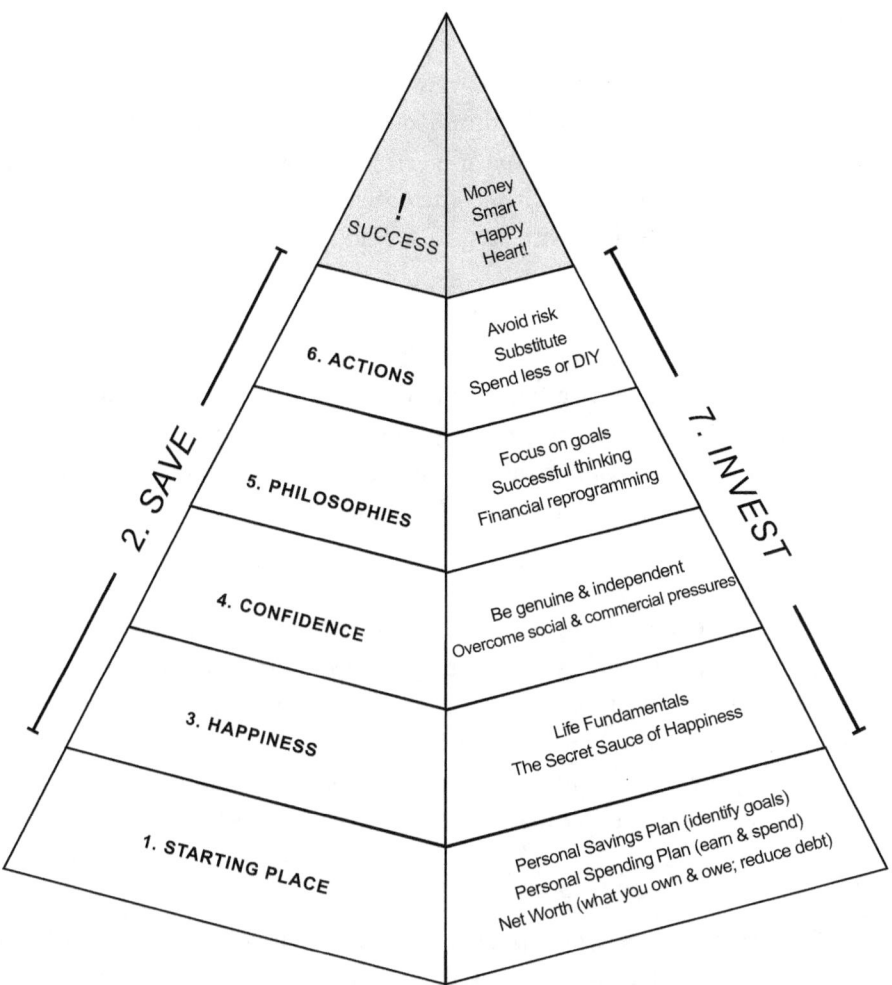

Step 1

STARTING PLACE: Establish your starting place by finding your Net Worth: what you own and what you owe then determine how to reduce your debt. Complete your Personal Spending Plan: what you earn less what you spend now and what changes you will make for Smart Spending. (Chapter 3) Identify your financial dreams and fill out your Personal Savings Plan: how much they cost, how much you can save toward each, and how long until they're yours. (Chapter 2)

Step 2

SAVE: Keep your money yours and grow rich over time. If you follow the guidance in this book, you will minimize your expenses and get that good feeling knowing you are doing what it takes to achieve financial security. You can now answer the question in the Introduction, "I Know I Should Save... But HOW?" Answer: "I do it with steps 3-6 below."

Step 3

HAPPINESS: Drink it in. Smother yourself in The Secret Sauce of Happiness. Use authentic happiness as a tool to build your financial success by living a fun, fulfilling life, experiencing the joy money just can't buy. Uncover the foundation of your most satisfying life, through the Personal Evaluation: Life Fundamentals exercises—then make it happen. (Chapter 2)

Step 4

CONFIDENCE: Conduct your financial life with confidence. Overcome societal, commercial, and your own pressures around personal worth, success, and money by "Busting Your Buts" and accepting yourself—who you are and where you are—right now. Feel your strength. Feel the power of who you are. Live your most genuine and independent life, true to you, spending smart and loving yourself because of it. (Chapters 1, 4 & 5)

Step 5

PHILOSOPHIES: Since your beliefs lead to your behaviors, believe in yourself and adopt the philosophies throughout this book. Change the way you relate to money and reprogram your mind to see yourself as financially savvy. Think like the successful people who are living happy, modest lives and are quietly growing a fortune behind the scenes. Focus on your goals, not the distractions that keep you further from them. (Chapters 1, 4 & 5)

Step 6

ACTIONS: Your actions shape your life, so act like the working rich who rise above the chatter, live below their means, and end up retiring in comfort and having the big things they really want. Employ money-smart strategies by spending less, doing it yourself, substituting, and avoiding risky situations. (Chapters 1, 4 & 5)

Step 7

INVEST: Once the cash starts to accumulate, turbo charge it with a compounding investment. I leave the investing advice to the experts; however, a simple primer to get you familiar with some basic investing terms and concepts is presented in the next chapter. (Chapter 6)

The result:

SUCCESS! Step by step, climb the pyramid until you reach the top. You can have it all: the happiness money will never buy and the big things it can. This is *Money Smart, Happy Heart* success!

You can do it!

The power is yours.

As Morpheus says in *The Matrix*, "I'm trying to free your mind...But I can only show you the door. You're the one that has to walk through it."

Chapter 6

INVESTMENT BRIEFS

The focus of this book is to help get you to the end of every month with money to save. Investing your money is the next step—to make it grow. I now want to help you acquire a basic knowledge of investing, so when you speak with a professional, or do further research on your own, you will have a basis for understanding the concepts. I am not an investment advisor, nor am I an investment expert, but I can point you in a direction to learn more. This chapter provides a simple introduction to some investment basics.

If you have ever spoken with a professional financial planner, stockbroker, investment advisor, or heard market reports, you might have gone away with the idea that the stock market and world of investing is a complex, confusing and scary place. And, actually, it is.

IT'S COMPLEX because it encompasses thousands of companies that produce millions of products and services of every type imaginable (and more you couldn't imagine). It spans the globe and deals with hundreds of countries, their economic conditions, and currencies.

IT'S CONFUSING because not only does it have its own language and lingo, the entirety of it cannot be completely mastered even if you have years of study and experience. Micro and macro economic situations and governmental policies in every country on the planet affect the market. The stock market has so many variables and is so complex and unpredictable that there is not one person on this good green Earth who can accurately and consistently predict what it will do—not even the Muckiest Mucks on Wall Street. I call the stock market "The Great Equalizer." We've all got just about the same chance (if we know and apply some basics).

IT'S SCARY because people can and do lose large amounts of money. To minimize the chances of this happening to you, you must understand certain concepts.

But there is another kinder, gentler side of investing. A side where flowers grow, the sun shines and people are very, very happy. Do people get rich by investing in the stock market? Yes. Can you? I plan to. Does it happen overnight? Well, if you have a lot to start with, an iron stomach and a whole lot of luck, then maybe. The other, and often recommended, approach is to be patient. It can take years of slow and steady growth. You can put a million dollars into the stock market and lose it overnight. Or, you can put a thousand dollars into the market and grow it into a million over years. If you make a one-time investment of only $1,000 and earn a 10 percent return annually, it will grow to become one million dollars in 73 years. Although that may seem like a long time, where else can you drop off a thousand bucks, sit on your porch and drink lemonade, then come back and collect a million?[24]

SOME BASIC INVESTING TERMS AND CONCEPTS:

INVESTMENT VEHICLES

"Investment Vehicle" is just a fancy phrase describing "an investment where you put your money." Stocks, bonds, mutual funds, savings accounts, commodities, and commercial paper are all "investment vehicles." Use this phrase like an expert by asking an investment advisor, "What investment vehicles do you recommend?"

---

[24] PARENTS! If you invest only $2,000 the day your child is born, never add another dime to it, keep it there and never touch it or allow your child to touch it until he or she reaches age 65, with a 10% annual return, before paying taxes, your little investment would grow to over $980,000! Tell him to buy his own car. She can pay for her own wedding. But down the road, you will be giving a gift of love, security, freedom, and money beyond their wildest dreams.

STOCK

When you buy stock you become a part owner of a company. An owner of stock is called a "shareholder" and the company is considered "publicly held." You can *sell* your stock *to* other people who want to own it, or you can *buy* stock *from* other people who already own it. If more people want to buy the stock than sell it, the price of the stock goes up. But, if more people want to sell the stock than buy it, the price goes down.

Often, if you buy stock in a company and the company makes more money than is expected, the price of the stock will go up. If the company performs worse than is expected, the price of the stock will go down. Ironically, a company might make a big profit in a quarter and still see its stock price go down. Why? Because the Wall Street analysts expected the company to make even more profits than it did. Thus, it did not live up to expectations.

The price of a stock can be influenced by many other factors aside from expectations. But, boiled down to the basics, stock, like any other product, is priced according to supply and demand. Regardless if the price of a stock is rising or falling, if the company is making enough profits to share with its owners, you may also receive a dividend. (Dividends are explained below under "Dividends and Distributions.")

EQUITY

"Equity" simply means ownership. Someone who asks, "How much equity do you have in your house?" is asking how much is your home worth on the market today minus how much you still owe on your loan to the bank (your mortgage). The owners of a company have "equity" in the company. If you and a partner start a company and you own 40% of it and your partner owns 60% of it, you would have "40% ownership equity." If you buy one share of stock in a publicly traded company, you would have a very tiny "ownership equity" (because companies often have millions of shares of stock).

SECURITIES

"Securities" are a type of investment: a stock or a bond (or a stock option, which is a more complex arrangement, that we won't get into here). To describe an investment where you loan your money and you get paid interest (bonds, money markets, certificate of deposits, etc.), the term "debt security" applies, whereas "equity securities" means you own a part of a corporation (e.g., stock).

MUTUAL FUNDS

A "mutual fund" is a collection of individual investments that share a common goal. It works like this: a bunch of stocks or bonds or other investments are purchased and thrown into a pool or "fund." When you buy one share of that fund, you are buying a small portion of every investment in that fund. Because some stock prices will rise and others will fall, by buying a little bit of each you are reducing the risk of your investment sharply declining in value. Although individual stocks may bounce up and down radically, the average of the group of stocks in a fund would rise and fall, but not so severely. Thus, owning a small piece of many different stocks limits downside losses. Does this strategy limit your upside potential, too? Yes, it does. This is where free will, your own judgment, and the relative thickness of your stomach lining comes into play. If you are a risk-taker and can calmly weather the ups and downs (sometimes the down, down, downs) of individual stock, perhaps that is the way to go. If your gut is a bit softer, mutual funds help to spread the risk but still keep you in the historically relatively high-earning stock market. My intention here is not to give investment advice. You need to talk to a reputable and reliable investment expert who will give you individual advice based on your unique situation or learn about the choices yourself.

Investments that are held in a mutual fund have some commonality. A mutual fund, like the investments held within the fund, share a common goal. That is for, either:

1. Growth - stock of a company that is expected to be successful, profitable, and go up

2. Value - buying stock of a company that is undervalued and waiting until its value is recognized by the market and then the price will go up

3. Protection - buying investments that will keep your money safe

In addition to sharing one of those goals listed above, a mutual fund is made up of investments of a similar type.

Examples of that investment type are:

- Stocks of a certain industry, e.g., high tech, banking, health care, communications, etc. ("Sector Funds")

- Stocks from huge well-established companies ("Large Capitalization" aka "Large Cap" Funds)

- Stocks from small or start up companies ("Small Capitalization" aka "Small Cap" Funds)

- Stocks from companies based around the world ("Global" or "International" Funds)

- A mix of stocks that represent one of the major market indexes like the Dow Jones Industrial Average, the S&P 500, the Wilshire 5,000, etc. ("Index Funds")

- A mix of bonds (not surprisingly called a "Bond Fund")

- A combination of stocks and bonds or cash ("Balanced Fund")

Although the fund has a mandate to fulfill its stated objective, some only have to invest a minimum percentage (for example, 80%) of the portfolio to directly achieve that goal. The remaining amount may be invested in something completely different, like options, futures, foreign securities, currencies, etc.

Every mutual fund has a "Money Manager," either one individual or a team of people who decide what to buy and sell within the fund, how long to hold onto each investment and the strategy on how to best achieve their goals. If you want to learn more about one of the thousands of funds available, read through its "prospectus." This is a report that will tell you about the fund's goals and strategies, risks, past performance, fees and expenses, management and other financial information. Every prospectus will tell you, "Past performance is not a predictor of future results." This is evidence of the "Great Equalizer" at work. You can't assume that just because a mutual fund (or a stock) has done well in the past, it will keep up those same results.

BONDS

A "bond" is a loan to a company or government. When you buy a bond, you give your money to the entity that needs cash. In return you get a document that states you'll receive your loan back at a certain date (its "maturity" date), how much interest you'll be paid and how often.

The interest rate you receive on a bond varies according to the risk associated with the borrower. If the federal government is the borrower (bonds called "Treasuries"), the risk is very low that you will not get your principal back. Therefore, the interest rate you will be paid is lower than others. This is generally considered the "risk-free" rate. A high-risk bond, which carries a high interest rate, is called a "junk bond." This is a loan to a company that has a higher probability of defaulting on your loan (not paying you back) . Bonds that fall between the highest and lowest return rates are "Muni's" or "Municipal Bonds" (state and local government bonds) and corporate bonds.

Typically, when you receive interest on an investment, you will have to pay federal, state and possibly local income taxes on the interest. The exceptions are muni bonds and treasuries. Because some income taxes are waived on the interest you'll receive on these investments, your after-tax yield may be higher than other bonds with higher stated interest rates.

CERTIFICATES OF DEPOSIT (CD)

Issued by a bank or a savings and loan, a CD is a loan to a financial institution. You can invest in a CD for as little as 30, 60, or 90 days, or for years. The longer you allow the bank to hold onto your cash, the higher the rate they'll pay you. Your money is generally safe; check if it is backed by the Federal Deposit Insurance Corporation (FDIC), a government agency that will pay you back your principal (generally, up to $250,000, but ask about specifics as they apply to your situation) in case your bank goes out of business or otherwise defaults on your loan. (See fdic.gov for more on government-backed insurance.)

MONEY MARKET FUND
(Also referred to simply as a MONEY MARKET)

When you invest in a "money market," you are buying shares in a mutual fund that only holds relatively short-term investments. Unlike many mutual funds, a money market does not buy stock, but similar to other mutual funds, it will use the benefit of the large amount of pooled cash (from you and many other investors) to buy investments an individual would generally not otherwise have access to. The price of one share is almost always $1. You can pull your money out of a money market at will, making it extremely liquid. You are often able to write checks from your account as well.

WHAT OTHER TYPES OF INVESTMENTS ARE THERE?

There are hundreds of ways to invest. You can buy foreign currencies, penny stocks or pork bellies. You can be a partner in a major real estate venture or you can procure futures, options, commodities, subordinated debentures, precious metals or part interest in a racehorse. This is an introduction to some common investments. I wouldn't get involved with less common, more sophisticated investments unless I've researched them fully and understand the risks involved completely.

STOCK MARKET AND STOCK EXCHANGES

Stocks are bought and sold through the exchanges. The two major American stock exchanges are the New York Stock Exchange (NYSE) and the Nasdaq stock exchange. The NYSE is considered to trade stock from mostly larger stable corporations, where the Nasdaq is generally known for trading stock from smaller and technology-oriented companies (though it also trades larger and non-tech companies). These exchanges are companies themselves that allow the flow of stock to be traded. All stock being traded through all sources is considered the stock market.

MARKET INDEX

An index is a basket or a group of securities that together track the performance of a particular section of the economy, industry or the entire stock market as a whole. They are often a group of stocks that share something in common, such as company size (small, medium or large) or sector, meaning the type of business or product made by the underlying company, like technology or healthcare. Taken together, the group of stocks, or index, is meant to represent the broader market and tracks how it is behaving—going up or going down—over time.

In Paula Pant's terrific article, "The S&P 500, NASDAQ, Dow Jones - What is This Stuff? What Is a Market Index? What Does It Represent[25]?" she describes, "the most popular market indexes" as follows:

The S&P 500 – This index tracks 500 large U.S. companies across a wide span of industries and sectors. The stocks in the S&P 500 represent roughly 70 percent of all the stocks that are publicly traded. "S&P" stands for "Standard and Poor's," the name of a market research firm. Companies CAN be listed in more than one index. Some of the largest companies within the S&P 500 are also in the Dow Jones Industrial Average.

The Dow Jones Industrial Average – Named after Charles Dow, this index tracks the 30 largest U.S. companies. This means it represents "large-cap" companies, which is the industry term for "very big companies" like Johnson & Johnson, McDonalds and Coca-Cola. Although the companies within the Dow Jones represent only about 25 percent of all stocks, the DJIA is widely accepted as the leading indicator of market health.

The Wilshire 5000 – This index represents up to 5,000 companies of all shapes and sizes, from gigantic corporations to the smallest of small companies. (In industry-terminology, these are known as "large cap," "mid-cap" and "small-cap.") The Wilshire 5000 is often called the "total market index." Strangely, despite how representative this index is, it isn't nearly as popular or as followed as the DJIA and S&P 500.

The Russell 2000 – The Dow Jones focuses on large companies, but the Russell 2000 does the opposite: it tracks only the smallest companies. This index follows 2,000 of the smallest players in the stock market. If you think that 2,000 companies is too small of a sample size, and you're searching for a larger, more representative snapshot of how small-cap companies are faring, you can also check out its sister index, the Russell 3000.

---

25 URL of Paula Pant's article: http://budgeting.about.com/od/budget_definitions/a/The-S-and-p-500-Nasdaq-Dow-Jones-market-index.htm Date of article's creation or publication is not provided on the article.

The NASDAQ – I saved this one for last because it can get a little confusing. "Nasdaq" refers to both an index and a trading exchange. Let me back up a little and give you some background: There's a marketplace where people go to buy stocks. This marketplace is called an "exchange." The most famous one is the New York Stock Exchange. There's also a famous one called the Nasdaq Exchange. Stocks that are traded on the Nasdaq Exchange tend to be tech companies, like Apple and Google. Of course, companies on the Nasdaq don't have to be as huge as those two icons. Smaller companies like Angie's List (the website that offers peer-to-peer reviews of home-repair contractors) and 1-800-Flowers (the website that delivers flowers) are also listed on the Nasdaq exchange. The Nasdaq also trades some banking companies, airline companies like Spirit Airlines, and even a few non-tech businesses like Starbucks and shoe company Steve Madden. In other words, there's no cast-in-stone law that says only high-tech companies are traded on the Nasdaq Exchange. The Nasdaq just *generally* tends to hold an abundance of tech companies. The Nasdaq market index, which is known as the "Nasdaq Composite," tracks the roughly 3,000 companies that are traded on the Nasdaq exchange. This is unusual, because no other exchange has its own popular index. The nightly news doesn't read stats from the "New York Stock Exchange Composite." The Nasdaq Composite has grown popular because it's commonly accepted as a shorthand indicator of how tech-sector and innovative companies—both big and small—are faring."

INDEX (MUTUAL) FUNDS

The Vanguard Group, a large and respected investment management company that offers mutual funds, defines index mutual funds this way:

"Instead of hiring fund managers to actively select which stocks or bonds the fund will hold, an index fund buys all (or a representative sample) of the securities in a specific index, like the S&P 500 Index. The goal of an index fund is to track the performance of a specific market benchmark as closely as possible. That's why you may hear it referred to as a "passively managed" fund."

EXCHANGE-TRADED FUNDS (ETF)

Similar to a mutual fund, an ETF is a collection of securities that represent an index. ETFs are traded on a stock exchange like stock; you can buy and sell them at any time during a trading day (whereas mutual funds are only traded once a day). They generally have lower fees than mutual funds.

401(k)'s

In 1978, Section 401(k) of the Internal Revenue Code, a new and wonderful type of retirement plan, was born. This long-term savings plan allows you to defer the federal and state income taxes you would normally pay on the money you earn if you just received the money in your paycheck, instead of saving it in the account. Typically within a 401(k), you are given choices on how you want to invest your money. Choices used to be stock or bond mutual funds and a money market. These days more investments may be available (each company decides on the investments they'll offer in the plan). The interest, dividends and growth you earn on your investments within your 401(k) avoid current taxation. You will be taxed on your money when you take it out at retirement. The cash you withdraw is considered income to you at that time, and ostensibly you will be in a lower, retired person's tax bracket, so you'll pay less tax when you take it out later, compared to the tax you'd pay on it now.

Each year there is a maximum amount you can save tax-free in your 401(k). In 2016, the maximum contribution (amount you save) is $18,000 if you are under the age of 50. If you are 50 or over, you can save an additional $6,000 in your 401(k). They call this a "catch-up contribution."

As an added benefit, your company may match some percentage of the dollars you save (although they are not obligated to). Your employer may entice you to stick with the company longer by "vesting" the portion they add. That is, the money they put into your account becomes yours slowly, over time. For example, you may vest 25% of their contribution every year, so after your first year, you own only 25% of the money the company put in for you; after 2 years, you would own 50%; after 3 years, you'd own 75%; and after 4 years, you'd own 100% of their contribution. Thanks company!

Let's crunch:

Question - If you contribute $5,000 into your 401(k) and your company matches 25% of that, how much is your benefit? (Assuming your tax brackets are 21% federal and 6% state.)

Answer - First you save the federal and state taxes of $1,350 that you would pay on the $5,000 of salary if you didn't save it in your 401(k). Then, you get your employer's free money of $1,250. So, $5,000 gets you $7,600! You just made 52% on your money, and you haven't even invested it yet!

Another benefit of a 401(k) is that you may not withdraw your money from your plan before reaching age 59 1/2. If you do, you'll have to pay the taxes you cleverly avoided in the first place as well as federal, and possibly state, penalties. Yes, I said "benefit." You need help saving. By giving you fantastic incentives to put your money in and painful deterrents to taking it out, you're getting the help you need. (If you are between the ages of 55-59, check on special rules that may allow you to withdraw funds without paying a penalty.)

If the day comes that you absolutely need to access your nest egg for an important reason like to cover medical bills or buy your first home, if your employer allows it, you may be able to borrow money from your 401(k). You'll need to pay it back with interest according to the plan rules, but you're paying that interest to yourself instead of giving it to the bank.

If you have a 401(k) available to you, use it!

IRAs

If you don't work for a company that has a 401(k) available, you can get many of the same benefits by opening your own Individual Retirement Account (IRA) at a bank.

Like a 401(k):

- You still put away money for your retirement free from federal and state income taxes in the year you contribute.

- You may pay tax on the money when you withdraw it at retirement.

- You will pay a penalty and tax if you make withdrawals prior to age 59 1/2.

- You make the decisions on where to invest your money inside the plan.

- There are maximum amounts of tax-free money you can contribute per year.

Unlike a 401(k):

- You set up an IRA yourself through an investment house or bank, and it is not tied to your employer.

- There may be ways to withdraw your money without paying a penalty.

- There are typically more investment options.

If you have contributed to a 401(k) during the year, there are limits on how much you can contribute to your IRA within the same year.

A Roth IRA is similar in many ways to a regular IRA, the biggest difference being the money you put into the Roth IRA is taxable in the year you make the contribution, but the withdrawals are tax-free in the year you withdraw it.

The bottom line here is if you don't have a 401(k), contribute the maximum you are allowed to an IRA every year.

Both IRAs and 401(k)s follow IRS rules. They are, by their very nature, complicated and can be confusing. Sit down with your company's benefits department and/or a qualified retirement advisor to flesh out the details or do research yourself at irs.gov.

INTEREST

When you loan your money to someone, you get paid some percentage of the total amount you lend out. You can loan your money to a bank, a company, a city, a state, or the federal government. You will be paid a higher amount of interest if you loan your money for a longer period of time or if there is some risk that you will not be paid back 100% of your principal (your "principal" is the original amount you lend).

Some examples of investments where you lend your money and collect interest are:

- Banks - Savings Accounts, Money Market Accounts, Certificates of Deposit (CDs)

- Companies - Corporate Bonds, Junk Bonds

- State or Local Governments Bonds - Municipal (or "Muni") Bonds

- The Federal Government Bonds - Treasury Bonds, Treasury Bills or Treasury Notes (all called "Treasuries")

SIMPLE INTEREST

Getting paid interest on your investment then removing that interest from your investment account is called "simple interest." That is, the interest goes into a separate account, or into your hand. For example, if you invest $1,000 in a state bond that pays 10% interest once a year, at the end of year one you'll have your $1,000 of principal and $100 of interest. If you keep the interest separate from the principal, and you make the same investment again, at the end of year two, you will again have your $1,000 of principal and another $100 of interest. You are earning interest on the original amount you invested, only. This is a fine way of making money on your money. It's better than keeping your money in the cookie jar, but it's not gonna get you too far too fast.

COMPOUND INTEREST

The big money comes your way if you can exhibit these three basic qualities:

1. Patience.

2. Patience.

3. Patience.

Using our simple interest example, if you make 10% interest on your investment of $1,000, at the end of the year you'll have $1,100—your $1,000 principal and $100 of interest. Now, if you reinvest that $100 of interest along with your $1,000 original investment ($1,100), at the end of year two you'll make $110 in interest. That is $100 on your original $1,000 of principal and $10 on the $100 of interest from the prior year. Not only are you making money on your money, but you are also making interest on your interest. This is called "compound interest." If you continue to let your interest ride, year after year, something joyous and surprising happens. The interest you earn solely on the interest you never take out starts to grow by leaps and bounds.

Check this out:

In this example, you invest $5,000 per year and earn 10% interest. Look at the difference in the *interest alone* you'd have by taking out the interest each year (simple interest) versus keeping it in and making interest on your interest (compound interest):

Invested For	Simple Interest		Compounded Interest	Original Amount Invested same in each case: $5,000/yr
5 years	$7,500	versus	$8,578	$25,000
10 years	$27,500	versus	$37,656	$50,000
25 years	$162,500	versus	$415,909	$125,000

Viva La Difference!

The difference becomes more dramatic when we save *larger amounts* over a *longer time*.

Let's invest $10,000 per year and again use 10% interest. Wow! Look at the difference:

Invested For	Simple Interest		Compounded Interest	Original Amount Invested same in each case: $10,000/yr
10 years	$55,000	versus	$75,312	$100,000
20 years	$210,000	versus	$430,025	$200,000
30 years	$465,000	versus	$1,509,434!!	$300,000

How can you figure out how much you'll have by investing your savings? You can use a financial calculator, or go to an online calculator at fincalc.com, bankrate.com, fool.com or find another savings, compound interest or investing calculator you trust and input how much you can put away per year, what interest rate you expect to receive and how many years it'll be invested. Or, here's a way you can do it yourself with a normal calculator:

To find out how much you'll have at the end of 10 years by compounding an investment of $2,000 per year at 10%:

Punch in "2,000" in your calculator, hit the "x" key, then hit "1.1," then the "=" sign. Your result will be $2,200. Now, hit the "+" key, enter 2,000 again, then "=", then hit "x," and "1.1," and the "=" sign. Your result now is $4,620.

The result is the amount that, after two years of investing $2,000 per year, not taking any out, getting 10% interest each year on the investment and on the interest. You'll have—$4,620. To find out how much it'll be after 10 years, keep repeating these same key strokes 8 more times. That is, hit the "+" key, enter "2,000", then "=", then "x", and "1.1, and the "=" sign. Keep track of how many times you are performing the operation by counting out loud or making a mark on a paper.

By investing $2,000 per year for 10 years at 10% interest, you'll have $35,062.

What you're doing is this:

2,000 x 1.1 = 2,200

+2,000 = x 1.1 = 4,620

+2,000 = x 1.1 = 7,282

+2,000 = x 1.1 = 10,210

+2,000 = x 1.1 = 13,431

+2,000 = x 1.1 = 16,974

+2,000 = x 1.1 = 20,871

+2,000 = x 1.1 = 25,158

+2,000 = x 1.1 = 29,874

+2,000 = x 1.1 = **35,062**

If you want to know how much a *one-time* investment of $15,000 will turn into in 5 years at 7% interest each year, the calculation is:

15,000 x 1.07 = 16,050

x 1.07 = 17,173.50

x 1.07 = 18,375.65

x 1.07 = 19,661.94

x 1.07 = **21,038.27**

**Here's another good illustration
of the power of compound interest:**

Meet my two friends—Hans and Franz.

They are both the same age.

When Hans was 20, he started saving $2,000 *per year until* he was 30 (for 10 years).

When he reached the age of 30, he left his money in his investment, but didn't add another dime into it.

Franz started later, saving $3,000 per year *when* he was 30, but kept it up *until* he was 65 years old (investing for 35 years).

They both earned 10% interest per year.

Who do you think has more now that they've reached the age of 65?

Remember, Hans invested a total of $20,000 and Franz invested a total of $105,000.

Hans has more! He has $985,327! Franz has $894,380.

Even though Hans saved a fraction of what his friend did, because he did it earlier and had compound interest working for him over the years, he has almost $91,000 more to retire with.

Note: In the above examples and throughout the book, for illustration purposes I have used 10% or 7% interest. In a footnote in Chapter One, I pointed out the variability of interest rates, the fact that we don't know what they will be in the future and that there is no guarantee that you will get a return of 10% or even 7%, but at this point, it bears repeating. The stock market (S&P 500) has provided an annualized growth rate of approximately 10% over the last 25 years. (Data from http://www.moneychimp.com/features/market_cagr.htm, where they have a nifty historical returns calculator for the S&P 500. Put in starting and ending dates and it will give you the annualized growth rate over those years.) If you go to fincalc.com (under Investment Calculators, to: "The value of compound interest"), or another compound interest calculator, you can see the results of your own examples using different investment amounts and different rates of return. You can try more conservative interest rates like 3%-5%, until you have more information on the investments you pick and how much you expect them to return.

RATE OF RETURN

The gain you receive from your investment divided by the cost of your original investment, expressed as a percentage is your "rate of return" (also called your "return on investment," or "ROI.") This gain can be from the interest you receive on the money you lend out or the increase in the value of an investment. The concept remains the same whether you buy real estate, classic automobiles, art, jewelry, stock, mutual funds or put some money in the bank and get interest. If it is calculated and expressed over a one-year period, then it is called the "annual return." Unfortunately, you can have a negative rate of return, as well, if you sell for a lower price than you paid.

Examples:

1. You buy a car for $25,000. A year later, a car collector buys it from you for $30,000. Your rate of return is .2 or 20%. (30,000-25,000=5,000/25,000=.2)

2. You put $3,000 into a savings account at the bank. They give you $60 interest at the end of one year. Your rate of return is 2%. (60/3,000=.02)

3. You invest in gold by purchasing 1 ounce for $1,000. In one year you sell it for $900, less than what you bought it for. Your rate of return is -.1, that is, negative 10%. (900-1,000=-100/1,000=-.1)

CAPITAL GAINS

The increase in the price of an investment over the price you paid for it is its "capital gain." If the price of your stock goes up, you have a capital gain. If the price goes down, you've experienced a capital loss. A capital gain can be long-term, meaning the value has gone up when you compare it to the price you paid for it *over* a year ago, or a capital gain can be short-term, meaning the value has gone up compared to the price you paid for it *less than* a year ago. Generally, when people buy stock, they are hoping the price will go up. If they sell the stock after the price has gone up, their gain is the difference. This is also known as a "return." And, as you know now, the "rate of return" is the percentage of the increase compared to the original price. Example: if you buy one share of stock for $45 and you sell it a year and a half later for $52, your stock would have appreciated $7 and you would have realized $7 in capital gains (long-term capital gains, because you held it for more than one year), making your rate of return 15.5%. Taxes are generally paid on the gain you made on the sale of the stock.

DIVIDENDS AND DISTRIBUTIONS

Where do the profits of a company go? Well, the company may put the money back into the business by purchasing more machinery or making needed repairs or hiring more employees. Or, the company can take some or all of the profit out and give it to the owners. They call this type of money taken out by the owners of a *partnership* "distributions." The profits divided up and given to the owners of a *company that issues stock* are called "dividends." If you own stock, even one share, if the company does well and the type of stock you own pays out their profits, you may receive dividends at the end of the year.

LIQUIDITY

How easily you can get at your money is how "liquid" it is. If you are holding real estate as an investment and you want to turn it into cash, you must find a real estate agent, put your property on the market, wait for the right offer, etc. This investment is not liquid. If you tie up your cash over a set period of time, or you have to sell shares of stock and pay large fees to get at your money, your cash is not particularly liquid. However, if you have your funds sitting in a money market account, savings or checking account, it is quite liquid. (Greenbacks in a box under your bed are so liquid you might notice a steady gurgling stream of them winding their way into your wallet and out of your life.) How much of your savings should be liquid? Ask around and you'll get different answers. But basically, financial planners say to keep from three to six months of your monthly expenses available in case of emergency. They may also advise you to keep some of your money in cash instead of investments, if they expect the stock market to go down.

PORTFOLIO

This is simply your collection of investments. If you are just getting started, your current portfolio may very well consist of a stamp collection and your son's finger paintings. Throughout your investing career, your portfolio is likely to undergo many changes as you make purchases and sales. If you own more stocks than bonds, you can say, "My portfolio is heavily weighted with equities." If you own a condo and have a small amount of money in the bank, at your next affair as you pinch up a cocktail weenie from the hors d'oeuvre tray, you can declare, "Currently, my portfolio is almost 100% real estate." You don't even need to have any money at all to sound investing intelligent: "At present, I am in a period of building my portfolio."

"Position" is another fancy term you can pick up quickly. It just refers to what your portfolio looks like, or I could say, your portfolio strategy. Let's say you have finally got your finances under control and for the first time ever are starting to accumulate some money. Since you haven't decided where to invest your little cushion yet, you've got it in a savings account. Out to lunch with some coworkers, the subject of the stock market comes up. You might toss out there, "Personally, I have taken a strong cash position in my portfolio. Please pass the ketchup." Alternatively, if you have some mutual funds, a stock or two and let's say, a bond fund, you can throw your arm over the back of your chair and say, "I've taken a balanced position in my portfolio, comparably weighted between stock and bonds."

RISK TOLERANCE

Risk tolerance is a person's ability to handle swings in the value of his or her portfolio. Without understanding your risk tolerance, you may not be comfortable with the investments you choose.

There are two basic types of risk in investing:

1. taking on too much risk and losing your money, and
2. taking on too little risk and not growing your money.

I hate to be the one to break this to you, but this is the investment dichotomy everyone faces. To evaluate these risks, you should know about risk tolerance, diversification, timing the market, and dollar cost averaging. See below.

Question:

Which is the better investment?

- an energetic high tech startup stock that projects 40% returns (if it stays in business and you don't lose all of your money), or

- a flag-waiving Treasury that guarantees 5% interest from here until eternity (or its maturity date in 30 years, whichever comes first)?

Answer:

What's your Risk Tolerance?

One of the first things an investment advisor will do is to determine your "risk tolerance." That is, how much risk your stomach and your portfolio can take. If you are close to retirement age and don't have very much money, you may find that your risk tolerance is quite low. You don't have the money to lose or the time to make it up if you do lose some. If you can't afford to lose any money, you can't afford to take chances.

If, on the other hand, you're fairly young, you have a stash of cash and many more money making years ahead, you may be able to tolerate a lot more risk.

No matter where you lie between the two extremes above, before you make any investing moves, you'll need to understand how much risk you are comfortable taking. An investment advisor will ask you questions about your age, your income, your earning potential, how much money you have currently, how many years you have until you retire, your future plans, and how you would feel about losing some of your money, to get a feel for your risk tolerance.

DIVERSIFICATION

Once you have a feel for how much risk you can take, how do you apply that to your investment choices? You use it as a tool for "diversification," that is, how you spread your money out over a range of investments (each which carry with them higher or lower risk). If you can handle higher risk, that is, if you have the time, tender and temper, then you can allocate a large portion (for example, 80%), of your wealth to those high rolling stock and a small amount (the remaining 20%) to the regular Joe's of the market—bonds, CD's, money markets. Whereas, Mr. Play-It-Safe chooses to divide his investments by parking 50% in Treasuries, 25% in Muni's, 15% in equity mutual funds and 10% in cash. Depending on your risk tolerance, you can choose to diversify your portfolio in some percentage each of stocks, mutual funds, real estate, bonds, cash, etc.

Experts say that diversifying your portfolio is your most effective tool in reducing your risk. Mutual funds do this automatically for you. If you were to put all your money into one stock, your portfolio would be like a beach ball bouncing on the waves of your one investment, riding high some times and crashing at others. If you bought shares in a mutual fund, you'll experience much less volatility, since you would own a small portion of many stocks. Now, split your portfolio out among several mutual funds of varying industries, company sizes, and countries, and throw in a bond fund, include your home as the real estate portion and keep some cash liquid in a money market, and your beach ball will be safely floating among the ripples at sea, slowly rising and ebbing with the tides of the overall market.

The fancy lingo for splitting up your cash into different types of investments is "asset allocation." Cash is your asset. A senior vice-president at Salomon Smith Barney told me that 90% of your investing success has to do not with the particular stocks or bonds you choose, but with your basic asset allocation.

TIMING THE MARKET vs. TIME IN THE MARKET

Want some stodgy advice? Wear your galoshes when it rains. Eat plenty of fiber. Invest for the long run. Not sexy. Not particularly fun, just, according to many experts, good sound advice. They will tell you that if you want to have some excitement with your cash, either belly up to the craps table, or play a hand of timing-the-market. By all means, have fun with it. In my opinion, you should do it with money designated for entertainment. If you make money, all the better. If you lose it all in one hand, or one trade, finish your drink and shove off. It may be extremely short-lived fun, but hopefully it was a rush while it lasted. At least you know that your real security, your real savings, are growing slowly, year by year, and will be waiting for you when you need it. My understanding is that "day traders," people who time the market by buying and selling stock on a frequent, daily, or hourly basis, trying to buy when a stock is low and sell when it's high, overwhelmingly lose stacks of money. It's only that lucky one-in-a-thousand who gets his mug on the pages of Fortune Magazine as this year's hot trader. (When he really should be giving interviews to Lucky Bastard Magazine.)

A technique that you may find is a wise strategy for investing, yet still takes advantage of the market's ups and downs, is called dollar cost averaging.

DOLLAR COST AVERAGING

This is a simple method of investing where you purchase shares in an investment with fixed amounts of money at regular intervals despite the price per share of the investment. For example, I might choose a high tech mutual fund and invest into it by dollar cost averaging. I would purchase a set dollar amount, let's say $50 per month, of this fund. So, when the fund was at $10 per share I bought five shares. The next month it screamed to $25 per share; I bought two shares. The next month, it splashed back to $5 per share. I bought 10 shares. You are buying more shares when the price of the investment is lower and fewer shares when the investment is higher. Buy low, sell high. After three months of dollar cost averaging, per my example, I now own 17 shares of the fund at a fairly low $8.82 per share average price. This is also a time-conserving and brain-saving plan since you don't need to think or strategize about your next move in the market. It's set up in advance, working for you every month.

YOUR INVESTMENT STRATEGY

Although you will hone your own strategy from the research you do and/or the experts you consult, some financial advisors expound that where you invest your money, that is, what particular investments you purchase, is less important than identifying and implementing your overall strategy, which may include, among other considerations:

1. developing short-term and long-term financial goals,

2. determining how much of your money should be tied up in short-term or long-term investments and how much should be liquid (available),

3. assessing your risk tolerance (how comfortable you'll be with fluctuations in the market),

4. deciding on your assets allocation (what percentage of your money you put into different investments),

5. diversifying your portfolio appropriately (dividing your investments between different investments of varying risk),

6. making straight purchases or dollar cost averaging into the investments you choose, and

7. monitoring and adjusting your investments over time.

Once you have your basic strategy down, you will need to choose the precise investment vehicles for your portfolio. How does one choose a mix of stock, mutual funds, bonds, or other investments out the thousands of choices out there? Well, you can either learn as much as you can and go it alone, or you can enlist the aid of an expert. Which approach is best? That's for you to decide. There are two schools of thought.

One believes that as there are few things more important to you than your hard-earned savings, you have a responsibility to yourself to know, understand, and direct your own finances. Since neither you nor the "experts" can consistently compile a winning portfolio, you should trust and rely on your own judgment. Do your homework, save the fees and be accountable to yourself only.

The other philosophy is that there are institutions filled with people who do in-depth corporate analysis, track economic trends and have years of experience investing. Although they may not be able to outsmart every market downturn, they devote every hour of their business day trying to. If you are busy enough with the rest of your life and don't have the kind of time (or interest) needed to dedicate researching investment options, paying an advisor to bring his or her considerable experience and expertise to bear on your behalf may be a prudent decision.

INVESTMENT ADVISORS

"Investment advisors" or "financial planners" are financial experts who can help you choose and purchase investments, decide your asset allocation, and guide your general investing strategy. To find the right one for you, ask for references from your family, friends, colleagues, coworkers, accountant, banker, insurance agent, lawyer, or investigate on the web. The Financial Planning Association's website (fpanet.org) can help you find a planner near you. Interview at least three. Ask them all the same questions, including:

- What services will you provide?
- How are you paid?
- What are your fees?
- Which products or investments do you get paid or rewarded for selling?
- What other fees or payments are involved?
- What is your training and experience?
- What licenses or certifications do you hold?
- How long have you been in business and how many clients do you have?
- How do I get started working with you and if I want to end our relationship in the future, how do we do that and would there be any fees or penalties?
- What else should I know?
- Since I am talking to a few advisors before I make a decision to work with one, do you suggest I ask the others anything else in particular?

As you will be comparing these individuals after your interviews, take notes during your discussions and jot down how comfortable you feel with them. Your relationship with your advisor is very important. By interviewing at least three representatives, you will start to see different approaches, attitudes, work ethics, fee structures, and investment strategies. Only then can you make an informed decision on whom you should work with.

RESOURCES

Whether you use a financial advisor or you go it alone, becoming educated yourself is a wise idea. Sources of information abound: journals, magazines, newspapers, books, websites, television, radio shows, reports, and videos. Have discussions with friends, colleagues, investing groups, and in chat rooms. If you put your antennae up, you will tune in suppliers of information. Choose a few that speak to you and dedicate a few hours per month to educating yourself. Cultivate an underlying base knowledge and constantly update it. Although I do not advocate any resources in particular, financial writers and websites with more investing expertise and experience than I have, do. For example:

In the article "How To Start Investing: A Collection of Resources," by Trent Hamm, last updated September 15, 2014, found on thesimpledollar.com, he recommends both hard copy reading material and online resources. Full article URL: http://www.thesimpledollar.com/a-collection-of-useful-resources-for-learning-about-investing/

AAII's (American Association of Individual Investors) article "Best of the Net: 2013 Guide to the Top Investment Websites, 17th Edition" appeared in its November 2013 online issue. Full article URL: http://www.aaii.com/journal/article/aaiis-best-of-the-net-2013-guide-to-the-top-investment-websites-17th-edition?adv=yes

In Daniel Solin's US News & World Report online article "The Best and Worst Sources of Financial Advice, Check out these 8 great financial books, and avoid these 5 sources of advice," dated January 5, 2012, he recommends "8 great financial books." Full article URL: http://money.usnews.com/money/blogs/on-retirement/2012/01/05/the-best-and-worst-sources-of-financial-advice

Below are a few additional resources to get you started. Some are geared to beginners; others would have more advanced concepts and articles. Poke around on these sites for a wealth of information:

aaii.com - American Association of Individual Investors

about.com (click on the Money tab, then to Frugal Living or Investing for Beginners)

bloomberg.com

finance.yahoo.com

investingonline.org

investopedia.com

investor.gov - the US Securities and Exchange Commission resource & information

marketwatch.com

morningstar.com

motleyfool.com

nasaa.org - North American Securities Administrators Association

nasdaq.com - NASDAQ

nyse.com/data - New York Stock Exchange

A FINAL WORD ON INVESTING

The information on investing I am providing is intended as an introduction only. It is not intended to be comprehensive, complete, or investing advice. It is a simple primer to get you familiar with certain terms and concepts that will help you understand the further research you will do. There is much more to know about each of the subjects I have broached, let alone the entire wonderful world of investing. There is a wealth of information available to you. As I have said before, I am not a financial expert or advisor. I am, however, someone who has figured out what it takes to reach big goals and has walked the walk. Alongside my everyday working, living, loving, winning, losing, laughing, crying, daily life, I have lived the financial life described in this book. I have adopted the mindsets and philosophies and used the tools and techniques; I know they work. I am passionate about, and an expert on, how to find extra cash at the end of each month, what it takes to achieve financial and personal dreams, and motivating you to do the same.

SUMMARY

So, here you are at the end of the book and at the beginning of the rest of your life. You have a choice. You can put this book down, appreciate everything you have read, then run off to work, family, commitments...and continue life as normal. Or, you can take action to ensure your future. It's time for new perspectives and a responsible, respectful, successful approach toward money. Start now to build your wealth, security, respect and pride.

You've got the tools you need. You've busted your "Buts" and got your head in the right place. You have the keys to a fun, fulfilling, happy life. You've identified goals for your life and for your loot. You know that retirement isn't just a dream in the future, but will be real and you are the only one responsible for it being sad and subsistence or sparkling and secure. You know where you're starting from, where you're heading and how to get there. Move forward with confidence. Build your wealth by adopting winning philosophies and act on effective strategies, then make your money work for you by compounding your returns and structuring an investment portfolio to be proud of.

You now know how to be money smart and have a happy heart!

Start building your future today. I know you can do it!

> My story is perfectly true.
> 'Bout this smart guy who's rich 'cuz he knew
> to save up his money,
> and perhaps it seems funny,
> that this rich guy is soon to be...
> ...you!

If you enjoyed *Money Smart, Happy Heart*, **please write a review** at a Amazon.com

Connect with Cindy:

facebook.com/moneysmarthappyheart

twitter.com/cindytroianello

Visit MoneySmartHappyHeart.com for continued motivation, information and to help you build your financial confidence, happiness and success, and to:

Download the **forms** from this book.

Read my **blog** and join my **mailing list**.

Share your money-related experiences, challenges and wins at MoneySmartHappyHeart.com

- What makes you the most happy that has nothing to do with money?

- What is your best no-cost or low-cost fun?

- What are your biggest challenges and successes around money and saving?

- How do you save in a big way? What are your best philosophies and strategies?

- What did you learn from *Money Smart, Happy Heart*; what will you start to do differently?

Financial Coaching Programs are available at MoneySmartHappyHeart.com for:

- Individuals
- Couples
- Employees
- Workshops
- Groups
- Talks

REFERENCES

In this section, I have cited many resources used in the writing of Chapter Two, though this list is not all-inclusive.

TED TALKS:

Ricard, Matthieu. (2004, Feb.). *Mattieu Ricard: The Habits of Happiness* [Video File] Retrieved from https://www.ted.com/talks/matthieu_ricard_on_the_habits_of_happiness?language=en

Gilbert, Dan. (2004, Feb.). *Dan Gilbert: The surprising science of happiness* [Video File] Retrieved from https://www.ted.com/talks/dan_gilbert_asks_why_are_we_happy

Trice, Laura. (2008, Feb.). *Laura Trice: Remember to say thank you* [Video File] Retrieved from https://www.ted.com/talks/laura_trice_suggests_we_all_say_thank_you

Gladwell, Malcolm. (2004, Feb.). *Malcolm Gladwell: Choice, happiness and spaghetti sauce* [Video File] Retrieved from https://www.ted.com/talks/malcolm_gladwell_on_spaghetti_sauce

Etcoff, Nancy. (2004, Feb). *Nancy Etcoff: Happiness and its surprises* [Video File] Retrieved from https://www.ted.com/talks/nancy_etcoff_on_happiness_and_why_we_want_it?language=en

Hill, Graham. (2011, March). *Graham Hill: Less stuff, more happiness*

[Video File] Retrieved from https://www.ted.com/talks/
graham_hill_less_stuff_more_happiness

Csikszentmihalyi, Mihaly. (2004, Feb.). *Mihaly Csikszentmihalyi: Flow, the
secret to happiness* [Video File] Retrieved from https://www.ted.com/talks/
mihaly_csikszentmihalyi_on_flow

Brown, Brene. (2010, June). *Brene Brown: The power of vulnerability*
[Video File] Retrieved from https://www.ted.com/talks/
brene_brown_on_vulnerability

Brown, Brene. (2012, March). *Brene Brown: Listening to shame* [Video File]
Retrieved from https://www.ted.com/talks/
brene_brown_listening_to_shame

Killingsworth, Matt. (2011, Nov.). Matt Killingsworth: *Want to be happier?
Stay in the moment* [Video File] Retrieved from https://www.ted.com/talks/
matt_killingsworth_want_to_be_happier_stay_in_the_moment

Seligman, Martin. (2004, Feb.). *Martin Seligman: The new era of positive
psychology* [Video File] Retrieved from https://www.ted.com/talks/
martin_seligman_on_the_state_of_psychology

Dundon, Elaine. (2013, May). *Reject Rejection: Elaine Dundon at
TEDxHappyValley* [Video File] Retrieved from https://www.youtube.com/
watch?v=D4bkGC_2wNI

Achor, Shawn. (2011, May). *Shawn Achor: The happy secret to better work*
[Video File] Retrieved from http://www.ted.com/talks/
shawn_achor_the_happy_secret_to_better_work?language=en

ARTICLES:

Bratskeir, Kate. "The Habits Of Supremely Happy People." *The Huffington
Post.* n.p. 6 Nov. 2013. Web. August 2015.<http://www.huffingtonpost.com/
2013/09/16/happiness-habits-of-exuberant-human-
beings_n_3909772.html>

Hardy, Chrissa. "9 things to tell yourself when you need to silence your inner
critic: Positive self-talk works, because you don't have to believe everything

you think." *Happier*. n.p. n.d. Web. August 2015. <https://www.happier.com/blog/positive-self-talk-9-things-to-silence-your-inner-critic>

Ware, Bonnie. "Regrets of the Dying." *Hospice Patient Alliance*. n.p. n.d. Web. August 2015. <http://www.hospicepatients.org/five-regrets-of-the-dying-bronnie-ware.html>

Maran, Meredith. "The Activism Cure." *Greater Good*. n.p. 1 June, 2009. Web. August 2015. <http://greatergood.berkeley.edu/article/item/the_activism_cure2009>

Carter, Christine. "What We Get When We Give." *Psychology Today*. n.p. 18 Feb., 2010. Web. August 2015. <https://www.psychologytoday.com/blog/raising-happiness/201002/what-we-get-when-we-give>

Idler, Ellen. "The Psychological and Physical Benefits of Spiritual/Religious Practices." *Spirituality in Higher Education*. Vol. 4, issue 2. n.p. Feb., 2008. Web. August 2015. <http://spirituality.ucla.edu/docs/newsletters/4/Idler_Final.pdf>

"Music Soothes Anxiety as Well as Massage Does: Listening to relaxing tunes might be more cost-effective, researchers add." *USNews and World Report*. n.p. 19 March 2010. Web. August 2015. <http://health.usnews.com/health-news/family-health/brain-and-behavior/articles/2010/03/19/music-soothes-anxiety-as-well-as-massage-does>

Welsh, Jennifer and LiveScience. "Why Laughter May Be the Best Pain Medicine: Laughter with friends releases endorphins, the brain's "feel-good" chemicals." *Scientific American*. n.p. 14 Sept. 2011. Web. August 2015. <http://www.scientificamerican.com/article/why-laughter-may-be-the-best-pain-medicine/>

Cassano, Jay. "The Science Of Why You Should Spend Your Money On Experiences, Not Things: You don't have infinite money. Spend it on stuff that research says makes you happy." *FastCompany* n.p. 30 March, 2015. Web. August 2015. <http://www.fastcoexist.com/3043858/world-changing-ideas/the-science-of-why-you-should-spend-your-money-on-experiences-not-thing>

Pychyl, Timothy A. Ph.D. "Goal Progress and Happiness: How to decrease procrastination and increase happiness." *Psychology Today*. n.p. 7 June, 2008. Web. August 2015.<https://www.psychologytoday.com/experts/timothy-pychyl-phd>

Rubin, Courtney. "The Route to Happiness: Set ambitious goals, says a study." *Inc.com* n. p. 23 Aug., 2011. Web. August 2015. <http://www.inc.com/news/articles/201108/study-says-ambitious-goals-make-people-happier.html>

Poppycock, Susie. "The Only 3 Things You Need to Know About Money and Happiness." *Time.com. Everyday Money. Psychology of Money.* n.p. 28 Jan., 28, 2015. Web. August 2015. <http://time.com/money/3680465/happiness-and-money-study/>

STUDIES:

Shindler, Esta H. Editor. "Research oh Health and Social Networks." *The Framingham Heartbeat. Framinghamheartstudy.org* Winter/Spring 2009. The Framingham Heart Study in collaboration with Boston University. Web. August 2015. <https://www.framinghamheartstudy.org/participants/newsletters/spring_09.pdf>

Anwar, Yasmin. "Sleep loss linked to psychiatric disorders." *UC Berkeley News*. Press Release. n. pag. 22 Oct. 2007. Web. August 2015. <http://www.berkeley.edu/news/media/releases/2007/10/22_sleeploss.shtml>

Blumenthal, James A. Ph.D., and Patrick J. Smith, Ph.D., and Benson M. Hoffman, Ph.D."Is Exercise a Viable Treatment for Depression?" PMC. US National Library of Medicine. National Institutes of Health. HHS Author Manuscripts. PMCID: PMC3674785. NIHMSID: NIHMS386053. ACSMs Health Fit J. Author manuscript; available in PMC 2013 Jul 1. Published in final edited form as: ACSMs Health Fit J. 2012 July/August; 16(4): 14–21. doi: 10.1249/01.FIT.0000416000.09526.eb. n. pag. Web. August 2015. <http://www.ncbi.nlm.nih.gov/pmc/articles/PMC3674785/>

F Dimeo, and M Bauer, and I Varahram, and G Proest, and U Halter. "Benefits from aerobic exercise in patients with major depression: a pilot study." *British Journal of Sports Medicine*. Volume 35. Issue 2. Br J Sports

Med 2001;35:114-117. doi:10.1136/bjsm.35.2.114. n. pag. 14 Nov., 2000. Web. August 2015. <http://bjsm.bmj.com/content/35/2/114>

K Knubben, and F M Reischies, and M Adli, and P Schlattmann, and M Bauer, and F Dimeo. "A randomised, controlled study on the effects of a short-term endurance training programme in patients with major depression." *British Journal of Sports Medicine*. Volume 41, Issue 1. Br J Sports Med 2007;41:29-33 doi:10.1136/bjsm.2006.030130. 9 Oct. 2006. Web. August 2015. <http://bjsm.bmj.com/content/41/1/29.abstract? sid=9afd8676-f4fe-4dbb-aacc-c9111513d8bf>

Mammen, George MSc, Faulkner, Guy PhD. "Physical Activity and the Prevention of Depression: A Systematic Review of Prospective Studies." *American Journal of Preventative Medicine*. Volume 45, Issue 5. Pages 649–657. Nov. 2013. Science Direct.

Web. August 2015. <http://www.sciencedirect.com/science/article/pii/ S0749379713004510>

Hausenblas, Heather A. and Elizabeth A. Fallon. "Exercise and body image: A meta-analysis." *Psychology & Health*. Volume 21, Issue 1. 2006. DOI: 10.1080/14768320500105270. pages 33-47. Published online 1 Feb., 2007. Web. August 2015. <http://www.tandfonline.com/doi/abs/ 10.1080/14768320500105270#.VeClonioloh>

Pamela J. Goodwin, M.D., Molyn Leszcz, M.D., Marguerite Ennis, Ph.D., Jan Koopmans, M.S.W., Leslie Vincent, R.N., Helaine Guther, M.S.W., Elaine Drysdale, M.D., Marilyn Hundleby, Ph.D., Harvey M. Chochinov, M.D., Ph.D., Margaret Navarro, M.D., Michael Speca, Psy.D., Julia Masterson, M.D., Liz Dohan, M.S.W., Rami Sela, Ph.D., Barbara Warren, R.N., M.S.N., Alexander Paterson, M.D., Kathleen I. Pritchard, M.D., Andrew Arnold, M.B., B.S., Richard Doll, M.S.W., Susan E. O'Reilly, M.D., Gail Quirt, R.N., B.A.A., Nicky Hood, R.N., and Jonathan Hunter, M.D. "The Effect Of Group Psychosocial Support On Survival In Metastatic Breast Cancer." *The New England Journal of Medicine*. Volume 345, Number 24. © By the Massachusetts Medical Society. 13 Dec., 2001. Web. August 2015. <http:// s212373507.onlinehome.us/conferences/archive/2012%20fall/ pdfsfrommolyn/NEJMoa011871.pdf>

Thomas K. Houston, M.D., M.P.H., Lisa A. Cooper, M.D., M.P.H., Daniel E. Ford, M.D., M.P.H. "Internet Support Groups for Depression: A 1-Year Prospective Cohort Study." American Journal of Psychiatry. Volume 159, Issue 12. Dec., 2002. pp. 2062-2068. Web. August 2015. <http://ajp.psychiatryonline.org/doi/abs/10.1176/appi.ajp.159.12.2062>

Ferguson, Yuna L. and Kennon M. Sheldon. "Trying to be happier really can work: Two experimental studies." *The Journal of Positive Psychology.* Volume 8, Issue 1, 2013. DOI:10.1080/17439760.2012.747000. pages 23-33. Published online: 19 Dec 2012. Web. August 2015. <http://www.tandfonline.com/doi/abs/10.1080/17439760.2012.747000#.VeCjI3iolog>

Mehl, Matthias R. and Simine Vazire. and Shannon E. Holleran and C. Shelby Clark. "Eavesdropping on Happiness: Well-being is Related to Having Less Small Talk and More Substantive Conversations." PMC. US National Library of Medicine. National Institutes of Health. HHS Author Manuscripts. PMCID: PMC2861779. NIHMSID: NIHMS196280. Psychol Sci. Author manuscript; available in PMC 2010 Jul 1. Published in final edited form as: Psychol Sci. 2010 Apr 1; 21(4): 539–541. Published online 2010 Feb 18. doi: 10.1177/0956797610362675. Web. August 2015. <http://www.ncbi.nlm.nih.gov/pmc/articles/PMC2861779/>

Dunn, Elizabeth W. and Lara B. Aknin and Michael I. Norton. "Spending Money on Others Promotes Happiness." *Science.* 21 March 2008: Vol. 319 no. 5870 pp. 1687-1688. DOI: 10.1126/science.1150952. Web. August 2015. <https://www.sciencemag.org/content/319/5870/1687.abstract>

Sansone, Randy A., MD and Lori A. Sansone, MD. "Gratitude and Well Being: The Benefits of Appreciation." *Psychiatry. PMC. US National Library of Medicine. National Institutes of Health. HHS Author Manuscripts.* Psychiatry (Edgmont). 2010 Nov; 7(11): 18–22. Published online 2010 Nov. PMCID: PMC3010965. Web. August 2015. <http://www.ncbi.nlm.nih.gov/pmc/articles/PMC3010965/>

"Music changes perception." *University of Groningen.* n. pag. Web. 22 April, 2011. August 2015. <http://www.rug.nl/news/2011/04/058_jolij>

Heidelberg. "Spirituality Is Key To Kids' Happiness, Study Suggests." *Springer.com*. Jan., 2009. n. pag. Web. August 2015. <http://www.springer.com/about+springer/media/springer+select?SGWID=0-11001-6-805150-0>

Heidelberg. "Happiness is...looking forward to your vacation." *Springer.com*. 18 February 2010. Web August 2015. <http://www.springer.com/about+springer/media/springer+select?SGWID=0-11001-6-849021-0>

Ryan, Richard M., and Netta Weinstein, and Jessey Bernstein, and Kirk Warren Brown, and Louis Mistretta, and Marylène Gagné. "Vitalizing effects of being outdoors and in nature." *Journal of Environmental Psychology*. Volume 30, Issue 2. June 2010, Pages 159–168. ScienceDirect.com. Web. August 2015. <http://www.sciencedirect.com/science/article/pii/S0272494409000838>

Tsutsui, Yoshiro. "Weather and Individual Happiness." *American Meteorologicl Society*. Volume 5, Issue 1. January 2013. Yoshiro Tsutsui, 2013: Weather and Individual Happiness. Wea. Climate Soc., 5, 70–82. doi: http://dx.doi.org/10.1175/WCAS-D-11-00052.1 . Web. August 2015. <http://journals.ametsoc.org/doi/abs/10.1175/WCAS-D-11-00052.1?journalCode=wcas&>

Alcock, Ian, and Mathew P. White, and Benedict W. Wheeler, and Lora E. Fleming, and Michael H. Depledge. "Longitudinal Effects on Mental Health of Moving to Greener and Less Green Urban Areas." *Environmental Science and Technology*. Environ. Sci. Technol., 2014, 48 (2), pp 1247–1255. DOI: 10.1021/es403688w. January 7, 2014. Copyright © 2013 American Chemical Society. Web August 2015. <http://pubs.acs.org/doi/abs/10.1021/es403688w>

"11 Surprising Health Benefits of Sleep." *Health Magazine*. n. pag. Web. August 2015. <http://www.health.com/health/gallery/0,,20459221_11,00.html>

"Body's response to repetitive laughter is similar to the effect of repetitive exercise, study finds." *Science Daily*. Source: Federation of American Societies for Experimental Biology. 26 April, 2010. Web August 2015. <http://www.sciencedaily.com/releases/2010/04/100426113058.htm>

BOOKS:

Rubin, G. (2011). The Happiness Project: Or, Why I Spent a Year Trying to Sing in the Morning, Clean My Closets, Fight Right, Read Aristotle, and Generally Have More Fun. New York, NY: Harper Collins.

Harris, D. (2014). 10% Happier: How I Tamed the Voice in My Head, Reduced Stress Without Losing My Edge, and Found a Self-Help That Actually Works. New York, NY: Harper Collins.

Beck, M. (2002). Finding your own North Star: Claiming the life you were meant to live. New York, NY: Three Rivers Press.

FILMS:

Emotional Content, Iris Films, Wadi Rum Films (Producers), & Belic, Roko. (Director) (2011) *Happy*. (Motion Picture). United States.

Judy Tossell, Klaus Dohle, Christine Haebler, Trish Dolman, Phil Hunt, Compton Ross, Christian Angermayer (Producers), & Chelsom, Peter. (Director). (2014). *Hector and the Search for Happiness*. (Motion Picture). United Kingdom.

WEBSITES:

Authentic Happiness: https://www.authentichappiness.sas.upenn.edu/home

The World Happiness Report: http://worldhappiness.report

TED talks: https://www.ted.com/talks

Tara Brach Audio Guided Meditations: http://www.tarabrach.com/audioarchives-guided-meditations.html

OTHER:

Peterson, Christopher. (2011, Oct.) What makes life worth living (Part 1) [Video File] Retrieved from https://www.youtube.com/watch?v=DRiIAqGXLKA

Peterson, Christopher. (2011, Oct.) What makes life worth living (Part 2) [Video File] Retrieved from https://www.youtube.com/watch?v=SvZQsqHVjHU

ACKNOWLEDGMENTS

I would like to acknowledge the following individuals for their help and support during the writing and production of this book:

My husband, Greg—without his love, support, understanding and incredible artistic and technical abilities, this book would not be possible.

And to the following people for their moral support, encouragement and/or contributions to this publication:

Loretta Ames, Richard Brewer, Carmen Campeas, Cassie Campeas, Maggie Hanson, Jessica Kaye, Jennifer Kim, MS, CFP®, CMFC, ChFC, CLU, Penny Key, Carolyn Palmer, Milind Pasari, CFA, CPA, CFP,CA, Kris Raney, AVP, CFP®, CRPS®, Steve Rutledge, Laura Soloff, Chris Troianello, Tony Troianello, Kate Willard.

ABOUT THE AUTHOR

For over 20 years, Cindy Troianello has been helping people achieve their goals through individual and group coaching on financial, business, leadership, and work-related issues. She has trained groups ranging in size from 6 to 600 consisting of both American and international professionals in financial competencies, money management and critical business skills. She has taught at UCLA Extension, West LA College, numerous professional associations, as well as in many corporate settings. Cindy has a business degree from California State University at Fullerton, earned a CPA from Deloitte and Touche, and has managed accounting/finance and human resources departments in several Los Angeles-based companies. Her financial know-how, talent for coaching, training, and motivating are combined in *Money Smart Happy Heart*.

Contact Cindy at MoneySmartHappyHeart.com